
Country Distinguishing Signs

On several maps, international distinguishing signs have been used to indicate the location of the countries which surround Hong Kong. Thus:

(CN) = China

This book employs a simple rating system to help choose which places to visit:

 'top ten' sight

 do not miss
see if you can
worth seeing if you have time

Aberdeen's typhoon shelter and harbour

INTRODUCTION

Hong Kong entices from the first moment of arrival, plunging the visitor into an exhilarating miniature world of ancient Chinese tradition and 20th-century Mammonism.

These work together harmoniously: the pin-striped suited Hong Kong businessman, communicating with the financial capitals of the world from his 30th floor office, may consult a fortune teller on each important transaction. Buddhist monks exorcise a run of bad luck from the grounds of one of the most modern racetracks in the world. A geomancer calculates the exact hour at which the Hong Kong & Shanghai Bank's bronze lion statues may be safely moved. The contrasts are endless: luxury yachts alongside bobbing sampans; elegant

Essential
Hong Kong

by
JUDY BONAVIA

Judy Bonavia was born in Perth, Western Australia and
has lived in the Far East since 1962. She writes travel
articles and specialises in China's culture and minority
peoples. She has written guidebooks on the Silk Road
and the Yangtse River. She lived in China for a number
of years and speaks and reads Mandarin. Judy Bonavia
lives in Hong Kong.

AA

Produced by AA Publishing

Written by Judy Bonavia
Verified by Sean Sheehan
Peace and Quiet section
by Paul Sterry

Reprinted 1996
First published 1990

Edited, designed and produced
by AA Publishing.
© The Automobile Association 1990,
1994, 1994 (reprinted), 1995, 1996
(reprinted)
Maps © The Automobile Association
1990, 1994, 1994 (reprinted), 1995,
1996 (reprinted)

Distributed in the United Kingdom
by AA Publishing, Norfolk House,
Priestley Road, Basingstoke,
Hampshire, RG24 9NY.

A CIP catalogue record for this book
is available from the British Library.

ISBN 0 7495 0839 6

The contents of this publication are
believed correct at the time of
printing. Nevertheless, the publishers
cannot be held responsible for any
errors or omissions, or for changes in
details given in this guide or for the
consequences of any reliance on the
information provided by the same.
Assessments of attractions, hotels,
restaurants and so forth are based
upon the author's own experience
and, therefore, descriptions given in
this guide necessarily contain an
element of subjective opinion which
may not reflect the publisher's opinion
or dictate a reader's own experience
on another occasion.
**We have tried to ensure accuracy
in this guide, but things do change
and we would be grateful if readers
would advise us of any inaccuracies
they may encounter.**

Published by AA Publishing, a trading
name of Automobile Association
Developments Limited, whose
registered office is Norfolk House,
Priestley Road, Basingstoke,
Hampshire, RG24 9NY.

Registered number 1878835.

Colour separation: L C Repro,
Aldermaston

Printed by: Printers Trento, S.R.L.,
Italy

Front cover picture: *Night shopping,
Nathan Road*

boutiques and state-of-the-art shopping arcades compete with makeshift stalls and alleyway markets; skyscrapers peer down on old temple roofs; expensive restaurants disregard the food stalls on the nearby pavement, and residents of luxurious apartment buildings have little in common with shanty town dwellers and housing estate occupants.

Change is at the heart of this city-state. The ability to determine market forces and adjust rapidly to them applies as much to the street hawker with his barrow as to the manufacturing magnate on his factory floor.

The racy pace is set by Hong Kong people, eager to get a good job or open a successful business, provide for their families and, above all, give their children as good an education as possible.

To view Hong Kong Island from the decks of the

Star Ferry is perhaps your best introduction to this city-state of modern architectural masterpieces and giant neon signs.
Added to it all is the sheer beauty of the harbour, the stunning vistas and the tranquillity of its hillsides.

BACKGROUND

The discovery of pottery sherds, stone tools and iron implements in various parts of Hong Kong attests to an early occupation of the area. The natural riches of its land and sea encouraged agriculture and fishing, but its sheltered bays were the haunts of pirates. Harassment of settled communities and coastal trade became so intense during the Ch'ing Dynasty (221BC–206BC) that the Emperor ordered all inhabitants to withdraw from the area, creating a 'free fire' zone to eradicate the pirates. It took decades before the communities returned.

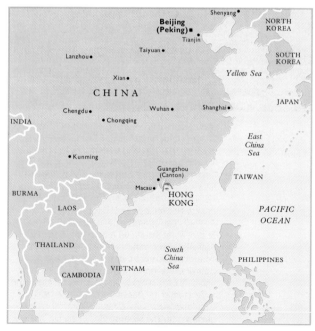

Crowds of worshippers come to make offerings of food at Kowloon's Wong Tai Sin Temple, built in traditional Chinese style

For many years, China cherished a unique and separate identity; Europeans did not begin to arrive until the 16th century. Even then, for more than a century the Chinese court was able to contain increasing European demands for access to the rich markets of China by confining their activities to the minute Portuguese colony of Macau. But by the 18th century 'factories' (warehouses) had been established at Canton from which foreign companies traded in China's silk, tea and porcelain, which were much in demand in America and Europe.

As the Indian opium trade, dominated by the British, Portuguese and Americans, began to drain the silver coffers of China, the imperial court became ever more alarmed at the deleterious effect of 'foreign mud' on its people and economy. Meanwhile, Britain clamoured for wider access to Chinese markets and was prepared to back its demands with impressive naval might. The Viceroy of Canton, Lin Tse-hsu, took the provocative step of burning the foreigners' chests of opium, setting the stage for the Opium Wars (1840–42 and 1856–58). A British fleet which sailed up the China coast and along the Yangtse River met with brave but ineffective resistance, and was able to impose the 1842 Treaty of Nanjing upon the humiliated Manchu Ch'ing court. This unequal treaty demanded a huge indemnity from the Chinese, the opening of treaty ports, and the cession to Britain of the island of Hong Kong. The convention of Peking in 1860 ceded Kowloon Peninsula and in 1898 the New Territories' 99-year lease was signed.

Hong Kong thrived, in spite of the malaria which killed off many a European in the first decades of the colony. It had become an important port for merchant and passenger ships along the southeast Asian trade route, a centre for careening and refitting vessels, and by the end of the century had an annual trade turnover of £50 million. Opium continued to be a major source of income, and the Hong Kong government's monopoly on opium processing in the colony continued until the late 1930s.

Its population was to swell with each successive upheaval in China and by the eve of the Japanese invasion in World War II numbered over 1.6 million. Hong Kong fell on Christmas Day, 1941. Many Chinese fled back to the mainland; others were deported. With the re-establishment of the British administration in 1946, the population increased by 100,000 a month, to be swelled yet again by China's civil war. The fall of Shanghai to the Communists in 1949–50 was to bring about Hong Kong's transition into a major manufacturing centre. Shanghai businessmen arrived with their textile, banking and business expertise, and their capital, and founded flourishing enterprises.

In 1984 the joint Sino-British declaration on the return of Hong Kong to mainland China in 1997 was initialled. This set the scene for long-term negotiations on the government which will represent the territory over the next 50 years as a Special Administrative Region of China.

Hong Kong's 413 square miles (1,070 sq km) supports a population of around 6 million. It is totally dependent on daily food supplies from mainland China.

Hong Kong's rich inheritance of culture and tradition is always apparent. This bridegroom's costume dates back to the Sung Dynasty

Away from the dense crowds of Hong Kong Island, the core of the colony, are areas still uninhabited by man. Hong Kong (including Hong Kong Island) consists of 236 islands altogether, as well as parts of the mainland bordering China: the Kowloon peninsula and, beyond, the New Territories, which also take in the 235 outlying islands. The diversity of these areas is what makes Hong Kong so special; a visit there is an unforgettable experience.

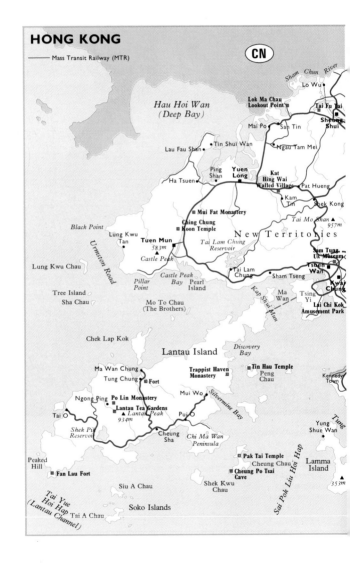

HONG KONG

—— Mass Transit Railway (MTR)

CN

Sham Chun River

Lo Wu

Tai Fu Tai

Lok Ma Chau
Lookout Point

Sheung
Shui

Hau Hoi Wan
(Deep Bay)

Mai Po

Sah Tin

Tin Shui Wan

Lau Fau Shan

Ngau Tam Mei

Ping
Shan

Yuen
Long

Kat
Hing Wai
Walled Village

Pat Hueng

Ha Tsuen

Kam
Tin

Shek Kong

Mui Fat Monastery

Tai Mo Shan ▲
957m

Black Point

Ching Chung
Koon Temple

New Territories

Lung Kwu
Tan

Tuen Mun
583m ▲

Tai Lam Chung
Reservoir

Sam Tung
Uk Museum

Castle Peak

Tsuen
Wan

Lung Kwu Chau

Urmston Road

Tai Lam
Chung

Sham Tseng

Ma
Wan

Tsing
Yi

Kwai
Chung

Pillar
Point

Castle Peak
Bay Pearl
Island

Kap Shui Mun

Lai Chi Kok
Amusement Park

Tree Island

Sha Chau

Mo To Chau
(The Brothers)

Chek Lap Kok

Lantau Island

Discovery
Bay

Ma Wan Chung

Trappist Haven
Monastery

Tin Hau Temple

Peng
Chau

Kennedy
Town

Tung Chung

Fort

Mui Wo

Ngong Ping

Po Lin Monastery

Silvermine Bay

Tai O

Lantau Tea Gardens
▲ Lantau Peak
934m

Pui O

Shek Pik
Reservoir

Cheung
Sha

Chi Ma Wan
Peninsula

Yung
Shue Wan

Tung

Peaked
Hill

Fan Lau Fort

Siu A Chau

Pak Tai Temple

Cheung Chau

Cheung Po Tsai
Cave

Shek Kwu
Chau

Lamma
Island

▲
353m

Tai Yue
Hoi Hap
(Lantau Channel)

Tai A Chau

Soko Islands

Sai Pok Liu Hoi Hap

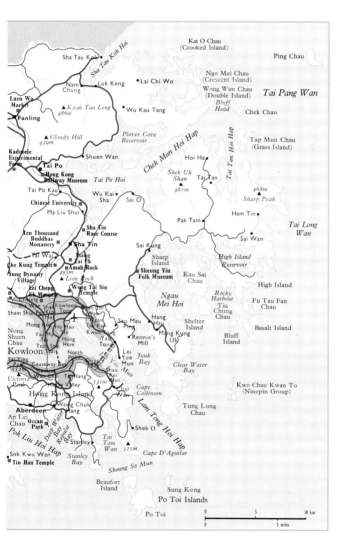

HONG KONG ISLAND

It seems scarcely possible that Lord Palmerston's phrase 'a barren island with hardly a house upon it', uttered in 1841, could actually ever have referred to Hong Kong Island, now one of the most densely populated islands in the world for its size – 2 million within 30 square miles (77·5 sq km). In spite of these astonishing statistics, it is possible to walk for hours through the island's hills where, at every turn, a magnificent view appears and peace and quiet reigns.

The population is sandwiched below the island's steep peaks, crammed along the coast, and creeping up the hillsides in high rise apartment blocks which lean and sway during strong typhoon

winds. For the tourist, the best way to imbibe the contrasting sights of the island is on foot – through the expensive shopping complexes of Central District, carefully down the steep narrow market streets of Western, or casually around the Peak with time to absorb the harbour vistas.

Causeway Bay's busy eastern corridor

CENTRAL DISTRICT

The Central District is the heart of the territory's business and banking world; its tower blocks ram the skyline and crowds jostle and swarm along the pavements. Air conditioned shops, boutiques and shopping arcades proliferate. The construction boom in the territory is nowhere more apparent than in Central, where giant office and shopping complexes are constantly under construction. Among the more spectacular is **The Landmark**, a multi-storey complex of chic shops surrounding a central atrium and fountain where exhibitions and lunchtime concerts are occasionally held. The 52-storey **Jardine House**, with its rows of porthole windows, has featured in the TV dramatisation of James Clavell's *Taipan*. Dominating the waterfront, the three towers of **Exchange Square** are most pleasing architecturally, and they house Hong Kong's Stock Exchange, as well as many major international trading companies and merchant banks. Beside the City Hall is another waterfront monument, the distinctive 28-storey Prince of Wales Building in **HMS *Tamar***, the Royal Naval Base, with its narrow, pointed base.

In the 1840s the district of Victoria (now Central) was perceived as a European preserve with Chinese areas to the east and west. This pattern appears to have been followed for the first decades more out of tradition than outright racism.

Three parallel streets dissect the area – Queen's Road, Des Voeux

Road and Connaught Road. The great business houses of Jardine, Matheson & Co, Butterfield & Swire, John Dent & Co, who dominated the China trade in tea, opium and textiles in the early days of the territory, built their trading headquarters along **Queen's Road Central** which, until the late 1860s, abutted the waterfront. Their company jetties and piers commanded the sampan-cluttered waterfront, and just below the intersection of Queen's Road and Pedder Street stood a public wharf.

Des Voeux Road – named after Sir William Des Voeux, Governor of the Colony from 1887 to 1891 – was constructed on reclaimed land in the 1860s and became the heart of Hong Kong's commercial district, with the island's first City Hall being opened by the Duke of Edinburgh, Prince Alfred, in 1869; soon the Hong Kong & Shanghai Bank and the Bank of Canton followed suit, establishing their headquarters in the 1880s. In 1927 Hong Kong Land Co Ltd purchased the Prince's Building site for £3 million, a princely sum in those days, when edifices in Bombay Gothic and arcaded colonial styles were popular. Further reclamation along the harbour front led to the opening of the **Connaught Road** in 1887. During the 1920s the scent of flowers pervaded **Wyndham Street**, also known as the **Street of Flowers**. Later the flower vendors were moved to **D'Aguilar Street**, where they remain today. The first English language newspaper, the *China Mail*, began publishing on

Wyndham Street in 1845 and so it also gained the nickname 'Fleet Street in miniature'.

At the top of Duddell Street a flight of granite steps leading to Ice House Street has been designated a historical monument and dates from the late 1870s. Four old gas street lamps adorn the flight and create a charming glimpse of old Hong Kong. **Ice House Street** was thus named after an American entrepreneur who began shipping lake ice from America by sailing-ship, and storing it here. On the corner of Ice House Street and Lower Albert Road stands a handsome red brick building built in 1904 as an ice house by one of the early Hong Kong companies, Dairy Farm. The building is now occupied by the Foreign Correspondents' Club and is treasured by its members. The Dairy Farm Company introduced a dairy herd to the colony in the 1880s, and it was said that 'nothing brought Hong Kong greater fame among neighbouring colonies and settlements where Europeans were gathered together in the East than the option thus afforded to her favoured residents of dispensing with tinned milk in their cup of tea.'

In 1911 Chinese fashion underwent an abrupt change, bringing another western influence to the fore. The streets of Hong Kong thronged with Chinese gentlemen wearing western clothes and foreign hats as they cut off their long hair as a symbol of solidarity at the overthrow of Manchu rule. Long gowns continued to be favoured

Flower-sellers were once based in Wyndham Street; now their wares sweeten the air in D'Aguilar Street

by the less western-orientated Chinese men, especially the intellectuals. Until the 1960s the graceful *cheongsam* was still worn by Chinese women of all ages, but unfortunatley, it has since gone out of fashion.

Walking in Central

A walk westwards along Queen's Road Central reveals the more interesting but less opulent life of Central District. Opposite Lane Crawford's Department Store (an old Hong Kong company which began as a ship's chandler) are two narrow, crowded shopping alleys (Li Yuen Street West and Li Yuen Street East) whose stalls

and shops sell handbags, belts, fabrics and a wide selection of clothing at attractive prices.

Upper Pottinger Street is one of Hong Kong's traditional stepped 'ladder' streets which appear in old, sepia photographs of Central. Its tiny stalls specialise in haberdashery items of every description.

Walking further west along Queen's Road Central, beyond the rather smelly Central Market (selling fresh meat, live fish and poultry and vegetables), and on towards Queen's Road West, the visitor will encounter an area of small lanes to the left and right. Here traditional Chinese life is in full swing, and a leisurely stroll in this area offers hours of intriguing exploration. Vendors selling the same goods cluster

HONG KONG ISLAND – CENTRAL

Just off Queen's Road, stalls sell a wide selection of items at attractive prices

together – vegetable and fruit sellers, flower and plant stalls, rice stores, Chinese herbalists, feather merchants and ship's chandlers. At 109 Queen's Road Central stands one of Hong Kong's oldest traditional apothecaries, the **Eu Yan Sang Chinese Medicine Company**. Its walls are lined with medicine cabinets whose drawers and jars hold thousands of substances made from plants, minerals and animals. The dispensers deftly dispense prescriptions, weighing each ingredient, be it bear's gall, lizard powder, toad cake, ginseng or tiger's bone. China's rich medical tradition dates back several thousand years and is still very popular, especially among the older generation. They feel that western medicine, though stronger, may have unknown side-effects, while the gentler Chinese concoctions are preventative in nature and accord with the natural body harmonies emphasised in Taoist thought. The store's display of ingredients are marked in English for anyone interested in the subject.

Shops in the area of **Bonham Strand** and **Hillier Street** specialise in the health-restoring ginseng root, known as the 'king of medicinal herbs'. The most expensive ginseng is gathered wild in northeast China, and only a very small quantity is imported annually into Hong Kong as the cost runs into several hundred thousand Hong Kong dollars an ounce. It is believed to have the ability to prolong life and is administered to a dying person, thus gaining time for distant family members to gather at the bedside.

Tea merchants displaying beautiful painted caddies of Chinese tea and black cakes of popular *pu'er* tea, also sell little reddish-purple teapots made in Yixing, a town famous for its teaware in China's Jiangsu province.

Be careful not to open the wooden drawers in shops in this area for they may contain highly venomous live snakes. Snake shops import snakes from China and Thailand for medicinal purposes and for nourishing winter soups. The snake's gall-bladder is believed to be beneficial to rheumatism sufferers. The skilfully extracted raw gall-bladder is swallowed immediately and chastened with a cup of wine!

Upper Lascar Road, better known as **Cat Street**, is an antique flea market where anything you can think of, from wood carvings and jade jewellery to watches and electrical appliances, is laid out on the pavement for sale. Redevelopment of the area is, however, slowly encroaching upon Cat Street. This was a heavily populated Chinese neighbourhood in the latter part of the last century, and when bubonic plague swept through the colony for the first time in 1894, the population in this area suffered the worst effects. Seamen awaiting berths frequented the drinking and red-light establishments here, to the chagrin of missionaries, one

of whom commented, in 1894, that 'they drink like fishes, ride round the town in rickshaws, making the night hideous with their shows, eat over-ripe fruit from street stalls, are stricken with cholera and die in a few hours.'

On **Tai Ping Shan Street** are three little temples which date from the mid-19th century. The **Kuan-yin Temple** is frequented by women praying to the Goddess of Mercy for the well-being of their children; at the Temple dedicated to the Pacifying General **Sui-tsing Paak** his healing forces are sought by worshippers. The **Pak Sing Temple** is dedicated to all ancestors, and means 'temple of a hundred surnames.' Over 3,000 commemorative soul tablets are kept here. Next to the Pak Sing Temple is the **Tin Hau Temple**. Tin Hau, the Queen of Heaven (or Goddess of the Sea), is a very popular deity and shrines in her honour adorn almost every fishing boat in the nearby harbour.

Hollywood Road is the centre of the antique trade and the shops display treasures and curios from all parts of southeast and northeast Asia. Artefacts include carved wooden furniture, golden gilded Buddhas, geometric neolithic pottery, sculpted stone lions, antique paintings, *objects d'art* of jade and ivory, and fine blue and white Ming porcelain. Even if you have no intention of buying anything, browsing among these lovely antiques is a delight.

The large Taoist **Man Mo Temple** (126 Hollywood Road)

dates from 1842 and, with its green tiled roof adorned with a frieze of porcelain figures, is a fine example of Chinese temple architecture. It is dedicated to the Civil God Man Cheong and the Military God Kwang Kung, whose statues stand side by side on the central altar. The air is pungent with the smoke and fragrance of the huge, smouldering coils of incense which hang from the ceiling. There are always worshippers visiting the temple to pray, light candles and burn incense. The sounds of rustling bamboo fortune sticks and clacking wooden fortune blocks are an integral part of the

mystical atmosphere which pervades this temple.

Lyndhurst Terrace also boasts antique shops, interspersed with picture framers and shops making the gorgeously elaborate traditional red Chinese wedding dresses, embroidered with sequins and beads, and golden jackets embossed with the queenly phoenix bird. They also make striking Chinese operatic costumes with accompanying high platformed boots and embroidered slippers. Towards the end of the last century, Lyndhurst Terrace became the address for a number of European brothels.

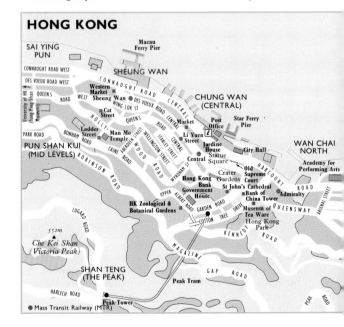

Historical memoirs refer to the ostentatiously daring behaviour of one American 'lady of the night' who received payment in signed chits. She would attend church once a year and place her unpaid IOUs upon the collection plate.

WHAT TO SEE

CHATER GARDENS
Chater Road
These stand on the site of the old Hong Kong Cricket Club. The Club stood in the very heart of the business district until the 1960s, occupying possibly some of the most expensive real estate in the world! So seriously was the sport taken that young expatriate gentlemen were advised to bring their cricket shoes with them from England and from 1866 regular matches were played with members of the Shanghai Cricket Club. In 1892 the ship carrying the Shanghai team home floundered in the South China Sea and almost all the team drowned – a tragedy the Hong Kong Cricket Club members took very much to heart.
Early each morning, people gather at Chater Gardens for traditional slow-movement *t'ai chi ch'uan* exercise classes.

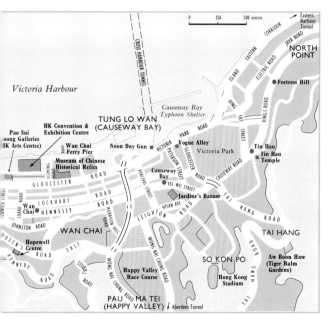

◆◆
GOVERNMENT HOUSE
Upper Albert Road
The official residence and office of Hong Kong's Governor, the Queen of Britain's appointed representative. Government House was built in 1855-6 but the Japanese added the oriental tower, roof corners and the portico entrance during their occupation of Hong Kong between 1941 and 1945, considerably improving its appearance. During the 1967 riots and disturbances in Hong Kong pro-mainland demonstrators were a common sight parading round and round Government House waving Mao's 'little red

The glass and steel headquarters of Hong Kong's largest bank – the Hong Kong & Shanghai Banking Corporation Ltd

book' of quotations. The gardens of Government House are thrown open to the public once a year, always on a Sunday and usually in March, when the azaleas and rhodedendrons are in full bloom.

◆◆◆
HONG KONG PARK
Main entrance: Supreme Court Road (near Admiralty MTR)
This 25-acre (10-hectare) green oasis in busy Central District is the territory's main pleasure ground. Numerous fountains and waterfalls intersperse a plant conservatory (the largest in southeast Asia), a vast aviary, visual arts centre, the **Museum of Tea Ware** (**Flagstaff House**) (see page 21), amphitheatre and restaurant.
Open: daily 07.00–23.00.
Admission free.

◆◆◆
HONG KONG & SHANGHAI BANKING CORPORATION LTD
1 Queen's Road Central
The bank's 47-storey headquarters were designed by British architects, Foster Associates, and this is considered one of the most interesting ultra-modern glass and steel buildings in the world today. There is an information desk on level 3 and 5 for those wishing to know more about the building.

The bank was founded by a group of China coast merchants in 1864 and has played a major role in Hong Kong's financial world ever since, occupying this site since the 1880s.

The three leading banks of the territory, the Chartered Bank, the Hong Kong & Shanghai Bank and the Bank of China, stood grandly side by side, since the 1930s, like imposing monoliths. Now only the old Bank of China, with its bronze Chinese guardian lions, remains for the present. Its new 70-storey home **Bank of China Tower**, designed by Chinese-American architect I M Pei, is nearby, containing the Tsui Museum of Art (see page 22).

◆◆◆
MUSEUM OF TEA WARE (FLAGSTAFF HOUSE)
Victoria Barracks, Hong Kong Park
Over 500 pieces of earthenware, porcelain, golden teapots, trays, ewers and bowls were donated by tea connoisseur Dr K S Lo in the 1970s for public display. He wanted others to enjoy his hobby. This museum

was created to house them in a delightful colonial style house originally the home of the Comander-in-chief of the British forces. The building dates from 1846.
Open: daily, except Wednesdays and some public holidays, 10.00–17.00. Admission free.

◆◆
OLD SUPREME COURT
Statue Square
Constructed in the first decade of the century, this building housed the Supreme Court until 1985, when it became the territory's Legislative Council Chambers.

Built in granite with tall Ionic pillars and a pinnacled dome, it typifies the English School of architecture and was designed by a leading British architect of the period, Aston Webb. It remains one of the few western-style old buildings to be preserved.

◆
ST JOHN'S CATHEDRAL
Garden Road
The Victorian Gothic-style cathedral dates from 1849. During World War II, the Japanese used the cathedral as an officers' club. The damage was extensive; all the early stained glass windows were lost, as were many of the memorial tablets. It has since been restored and is now a peaceful haven in the midst of high-rise Hong Kong. Lunchtime concerts are held in the cathedral once a week.

The nearby red-brick building at the top of Battery Path has had a very strange history. Built in the

1880s it first served as a junior mess for young bankers and traders, then as the Russian Consulate, before housing the **French Mission**, which was active in missionary work throughout Asia. Later the Education Department occupied it, and then the Victoria District Court. It is now designated to be the headquarters of the Joint Liaison Group, which is concerned with the 1997 return of Hong Kong to China.

◆◆
STATUE SQUARE
between Des Voeux Road and Chater Road
A small haven of green in downtown Central District, in which stands a statue of the Chief Manager of the Hong Kong & Shanghai Bank from 1876 to 1902. This area is the favourite haunt on weekends for thousands of Filipino maids who enjoy their day off work chatting and meeting with their colleagues. Nearby is the **War Memorial Cenotaph** and beside it the premises of the **Hong Kong Club** – 'once the paradise of the select, and temple of colonial gentility'. Today's modern structure replaced an elegant rococo façaded building built in 1898. Its demolition in the late 1970s was a source of much distress to those who fight the battle to preserve Hong Kong's architectural heritage. The area is closed to traffic on Sunday.

◆◆◆
TSUI MUSEUM OF ART
Bank of China Tower (11th floor), 2A Des Voeux Road
The dramatic Bank of China

Tower houses a collection of Chinese antiquities – mainly ceramics, bronze, carved wood and ivory and furniture. Many pieces are unique.
Open: daily, except Sunday and public holidays, 10.00–18.00 (Saturday until 14.00).

◆◆◆
VICTORIA PEAK

A trip to 'The Peak' on the Peak Tram is an essential part of any visitor's stay, for the ride itself is an experience (seats on the right hand side of the tram offer the best views) as the tram rises steeply up the mountain side, making the high-rise apartment blocks appear to be built on an angle. From the top the views are superb day or night. There are restaurants at the top which also houses the tram terminus and souvenir shops. It has amazing panoramic views.
In the mid 19th century Europeans took to building summer houses on Victoria Peak, 1,827ft (554m) high, and it became a place where 'one can spend a summer in Hong Kong with a reasonable probability of being alive at the end of it'. Elegant colonial houses sprang up along the ridges of Victoria Peak, Mount Gough and Mount Kellett, and in the 1870s the Governor, too, had a summer residence built here. Chinese were not permitted to build on the Peak until the turn of the century.
Access to the Peak, until the Peak Tram's construction in 1888, was by sedan chair, carried by relays of coolies. One eccentric resident of the Peak rode a

A view of Hong Kong from the top of exclusive Victoria Peak

camel! The Peak Road was completed only in 1924. Today an address on the Peak still has an élitist cachet, even though for some months of the year residents are shrouded in gloomy mist and cloud. Rents on the Peak can run to HK$80,000 a month.

A number of long scenic walks begin here but more leisurely and spectacular is the walk around Victoria Peak, along Lugard and Harlech Roads. It takes only 45 minutes and is quite flat. From this circular walk, among delightful semi-tropical vegetation, wide views of the eastern and western approaches to Victoria Harbour and across to the Kowloon peninsula are enjoyed, while Aberdeen and the islands of Lamma and Cheung Chau on the southern side of the island also come into view.

◆◆◆ ZOOLOGICAL AND BOTANICAL GARDENS ✓

corner Upper Albert Road and Garden Road

The gardens were opened in 1864, and the zoo section built in 1975. The lush aviaries are home to hundreds of species of spectacular birds. The breeding programme here has been especially successful, saving birds on the verg of extinction and supplying zoos worldwide with new stock. A statue of Sir Arthur Kennedy, Governor of Hong Kong between 1872 and 1877, graces the gardens. This is a very popular spot for family weekend outings. The zoo and aviary sections are divided by Albany Road, but are linked by an underground pass.

WESTERN DISTRICT

To the west of Central District, dried fish wholesalers dominate **Des Voeux Road West** in **Sai Ying Pun**, and the visitor's senses are assailed by the sights and smells of the merchandise – squid, fish, sea cucumbers, oysters, shrimp, jelly fish and abalone. Other delicacies, such as dried chrysanthemum flowers, red dates, dried mushrooms, lotus seeds and pickles are also sold. In the streets behind, wholesalers deal in sharks' fins and birds' nests – luxury items even for the rich Chinese. On **Queen's Road West** it is still possible to find professional roadside letter-writers. These calligraphers are in high demand at Chinese New Year to write red-paper auspicious couplets, which are pasted on the doorway of each Chinese home.

Calligraphy, developed in 200BC when the writing brush was invented, is one of the greatest of Chinese arts

WHAT TO SEE

◆
KENNEDY TOWN
Reached by tram, Kennedy Town offers a glimpse of the busy waterfront where junks and lighters load and unload cargoes from China. It is named after Governor Sir Arthur Kennedy (1872–77) during whose tenure wharves were built along the waterfront and middle-class Chinese merchants and craftsmen resided in the area. Take the tram all the way to Western and walk around Kennedy Town's market streets.

◆◆
UNIVERSITY OF HONG KONG
Bonham Road
Established in 1911, the University now has almost 8,000 students studying everything from arts to social sciences. Competition for places in this English language University is fierce. One of its most famous students was the Chinese revolutionary Dr Sun Yat-Sen (1866–1925), father of modern China. The original building, Loke Yew Hall, is built in Renaissance style around a quiet garden courtyard, surmounted by a clock-tower and turrets. The **Fung Ping Shan Museum** building, built in 1932, first served as the University's library before housing the Fung family art collection. The collection now consists mainly of early Shang, Chou and Han bronzes, neolithic pottery, glazed tomb figures and porcelains from China's famous kilns. The museum has the world's largest collection of Yuan Dynasty Nestorian crosses.

One of the fascinations of Hong Kong is the food – to eat or just to look at

Open: daily, except Sunday and public holidays, 09.30–18.00. Admission free.

◆◆◆
WESTERN MARKET
corner Connaught Road Central and Morrison Street
After renovation this elegant Edwardian red-brick building re-opened as a market in 1991. It is home to a variety of shops selling anything from hand-made dolls to teas. There are also food stalls and restaurants.
Open: daily 10.00–07.00.

EASTERN DISTRICT

The territory to the east of Central
District takes in the areas of Wan
Chai, Happy Valley, Causeway
Bay, North Point and Shau Kei
Wan.

WHAT TO SEE

◆◆◆
CAUSEWAY BAY

Prices in this busy shopping area
are lower than in Central District.
Big Japanese department stores
and a branch of China Products
are to be found here. A popular
local market in the area is
Jardine's Bazaar. One end
overflows with cheap clothing
stalls – blouses, jeans, underwear
– and the other with fresh meat,
vegetables, fruits and flowers.
Close to the bazaar is **Jardine's
Crescent**, with old-fashioned
shops selling traditional produce,
medicinal herbs and dried food.
On the waterfront, opposite the
Excelsior Hotel (accessible via a
tunnel under Gloucester Road)
stands Hong Kong's **Noon Day
Gun** which Noël Coward made
famous in his song *Mad Dogs and
Englishmen*: 'In Hong Kong they
strike a gong and fire off the noon
day gun'.
The custom had grown of giving
the *taipan* (a name by which the
heads of the major China coast
trading companies are known) of
Jardine, Matheson & Co an official
send-off with a 21-gun salute.
Annoyed by this arrogance, the
Navy directed the company, as a
punishment, to fire the gun at
noon each day until further
notice. The custom continued
until World War II when the
cannon was rendered useless.
After the war the Royal Navy

*The gardens that Aw Boon Haw
built are full of statues and grottoes*

provided another cannon, which,
in accordance with this odd little
tradition, is fired at noon each day
and on midnight of New Year's
Eve.
Causeway Bay Typhoon Shelter
is the permanent home of a
number of boat dwellers as well
as a haven for sampans, junks
and other frail craft when
typhoons threaten.
To reach Causeway Bay Typhoon
Shelter, walk over the overpass
near Victoria Park.

Causeway Bay abounds in eating establishments. **Vogue Alley**, located on Paterson Street (formerly known as Food Street), is an innovative shopping area featuring a number of boutiques selling designer clothes.

Victoria Park (47 acres/19 hectares) is one of the few open spaces in this built-up area and bird-lovers like to hang their elegantly caged songsters on the branches of the park's trees. There are a number of sports facilities in the park, and on Sundays it often becomes a forum for public meetings where local issues are voiced. People like to practise the martial art of *kung fu* or the sedate *t'ai chi ch'uan* movements here in the early mornings. A Flower Fair is held annually in the park at Chinese New Year, it is also a popular place to admire the moon at the Mid-Autumn Festival. The statue of Queen Victoria which graces the park was created in 1895.

The 'Tiger Balm' cure-all ointment millionaire, Aw Boon Haw, built the **Aw Boon Haw**

Garden in 1935 on Tai Hang Road. He filled the steep 8-acre (3.2 hectare) hillside above Causeway Bay with plaster statues which depict the whole range of Buddhist and Chinese mythology, much of it quite gruesome, especially the depiction of the tortures carried out in the afterworld's Ten Courts of Hell. The six-storey Tiger Pagoda is a distinctive landmark. The Aw family has a collection of jade, which may also be viewed.
Open: Aw Boon Haw Garden 10.00 to 16.00.

Admission free.
Bus: no 11 from Exchange Square (Central).

HAPPY VALLEY
Horse racing has been part of Hong Kong's sporting life – more as a passion than a sport – almost since the acquisition of the island by the British. The **Happy Valley Race Course** was created in 1846; when horses were imported from

A small street market in North Point, which is also known as Little Shanghai

Shanghai and northern China. One of Hong Kong's Governors, Sir Henry May (1912–1919), was both an owner and a jockey! During a race meeting in 1918 the stand caught fire and some 600 people perished. The racing season is from September to June (see also page 109).

Early attempts at settlement of Happy Valley were equally disastrous. In the early 1840s soldiers quartered here fell prey to malaria and the area soon became known as the 'White Man's Grave'. Even after extensive draining was carried out, epidemics continued to decimate the European population. Little wonder that the **Colonial Cemetery** was established here in 1845. The gravestones in this gently tended garden bear the names of many who were prominent in Hong Kong's early history and are a witness to the precariousness of life in the east – some died in typhoons, some at the hands of pirates and many of fever and plagues. John Le Carré recreates the cemetery in scenes from his book *The Honourable Schoolboy*.

NORTH POINT TO SHAU KEI WAN

Three districts lie east of Causeway Bay: North Point, Quarry Bay and Shau Kei Wan. In *The Hong Kong Guide,* published in 1893, the disenchanted writer makes the comment: 'The road to Shau-ki Wan was the Rotten Row of the Colony in those stupid days when everyone thought himself bound to keep a carriage, whether he could afford it or not, and the sole amusement was

solemnly driving along this weary road every afternoon!' Today these districts are residential areas comprised of both government and private low-cost housing estates. The Shanghainese clannishly settled in **North Point** and it is therefore also called Little Shanghai. Not surprisingly most of the restaurants here serve Shanghainese food.

Quarry Bay continues its industrial tradition. Dockyards were founded here in 1863 and later Butterfield & Swire, one of the leading Far Eastern trading companies which ran ships up and down the China coast and along the lower Yangtse River, built their Taikoo Dockyard in 1908. The Taikoo Sugar Refinery, also a part of the B & S empire, had already been constructed in Quarry Bay in 1882. The huge Taikoo Shing housing estate now stands on this redeveloped site, and the dockyards occupy a much smaller area.

Shau Kei Wan, at the eastern end of the island, in 1841 only a fishing village with a population of 1,200, still keeps its seagoing tradition. It is the homebase for a large fishing fleet, second only in importance to Aberdeen. Perhaps because of the poverty of its early villagers or because it was prey to piratical attacks, the area was known as 'the Bay of Hungry Men'.

There are two temples of interest: the **Tin Hau Temple** on Main Street, dedicated to the Queen of Heaven (or Goddess of the Sea) and built around 1874; and the **Tam Kung Temple** at the end of Main Street on the waterfront. On the eighth day of the fourth moon (in May) the fishing community holds boisterous birthday celebrations for Tam Kung, a deity who is believed to control the elements, especially typhoons. A beautiful 150-ft (45m) silk dragon dances down Main Street, paying its respects to all the business premises. Lively lion dances go on outside the temple throughout the day. Dragon boat races are also held at Shau Kei Wan during the Dragon Boat Festival (see **Special Events**, page 106). Take the tram from Central to Shau Kei Wan and catch the MTR subway back.

◆◆◆
WAN CHAI

Wan Chai is famous for its nightlife and 'girlie' bars, and never more so than during the Vietnam War when American servicemen came to Hong Kong for rest and recreation. Mention of Wan Chai immediately brings to mind the film *The World of Suzie Wong*, a poignant love story of one such bar girl. During the Japanese occupation (1941–45), Wan Chai was designated a red-light district.

But Wan Chai is also a respectable residential area, one of the oldest in fact, designated for Chinese occupation in the 1840s. Refugees from the bloody Tai Ping Rebellion on the mainland flooded into the area during the 1850s and larger squatter areas resulted. British military barracks were established in Wan Chai, just east of Central, and it was not long before brothels followed suit. A number of early missionary societies and church institutions built hospitals, mission

houses and orphanages.
Wan Chai still has the flavour of pre-war Hong Kong, with typical old four-storey tenements, sometimes with wrought-iron balconies and bamboo washing poles in evidence. But these too are slowly falling under the developers' hammers. As in Central, Queen's Road formed the waterfront in Wan Chai too, but reclamation during the 1930s extended the area to Gloucester Road. More recent reclamation has created valuable waterfront land for office accommodation, hotels, exhibition and arts centres, sports grounds and lighter cargo handling facilities.

Walking the small streets between Queen's Road East and Johnston Road the visitor will find street markets stocked with vegetables and fruit, bird shops, clothing vendors, and restaurants. You may also find people fortune telling, an occupation often practised by the blind.

On Queen's Road East the small **Hung Shing (Tai Wong) Temple**, with its carved granite balustrade, dates from the 1860s, while its Shek Wan pottery roof decorations are turn of the century. The big stone, around which the temple is built, is believed to have been a shrine even prior to the arrival of the British. Hung Shing is one of the patron saints of the seafarers. The 66-storey high **Hopewell Centre**, still on Queen's Road East, is one of the landmarks of Wan Chai: at the top is a revolving restaurant. Even if you are not planning to eat here (tel: 2862 6166) it is still worth taking the exterior elevator to the top for the panoramic views. The **Hong Kong Convention**

The Wan Chai red-light district is famed for its nightlife

and **Exhibition Centre** dwarfs everything in the area but its glass-front offers fine views of the harbour and Kowloon. There are several other temples in the vicinity, including the **Sui Tsing Pak** on Tik Lung Lane, which houses some interesting antiques, and the **Pak Tai Temple** off Stone Nullah Lane, dedicated to the God of the North and built in the 1860s.

The **Museum of Chinese Historical Relics**, on the first floor of the Causeway Centre, exhibits cultural treasures from China which include paintings and handicrafts: occasional exhibitions only (open 10.00–18.00; from 13.00 Sunday and public holidays; nominal admission charge). And in the Hong Kong Arts Centre, Harbour Road, the **Pao Sui Loong Galleries** hold regular exhibitions with particular emphasis on modern art (open daily 10.00–20.00).

MTR subway: Wan Chai Station

SOUTHERN DISTRICT

A trip along the southern coast of
Hong Kong Island is well
worthwhile. Several popular
attractions lie along this coast, as
well as a number of sandy
beaches.

WHAT TO SEE

**◆◆◆
ABERDEEN** ✓

Aberdeen's image has changed
vastly in recent years – from a
small fishing harbour to a modern
urban centre.
Fishing is still a major industry
and the harbour is busy with
deep-sea fishing boats. Many
Tanka boat people still live
aboard junks, and sampan
ladies importune tourists with
offers of 20-minute boat rides
(pay around HK$40) to see this
astonishing floating world. The
junks are quite spacious and
there is room for family pets,
chicken coops, drying fish and
the essential TV set. Sampans
selling groceries, vegetables
and fruit supply the floating
housewife with her daily needs.
The larger boats are fitted with
radar and make fishing
expeditions into the South China
Sea for several weeks at a time.
At Chinese New Year and the
Dragon Boat Festival the
harbour is packed with boats
bedecked with multi-coloured
flags and streaming banners.
Sampan rides around the
harbour are fun, and offer a
staggering glimpse of the
contrasts of Hong Kong's society.
Twenty-minute guided tours
leave from opposite the
Aberdeen Centre daily between

*Aberdeen Harbour, a floating
tourist attraction*

09.00 and 17.00 (tel: 2730 3031).
Your boat skims round and about
the floating homes and then out to
the vast floating restaurants, for
which Aberdeen is so famous.
These are moored beside the
opulent Aberdeen Marina where
the rich have their pleasure boats.
Aberdeen's **Tin Hau Temple** is
dedicated to the Queen of

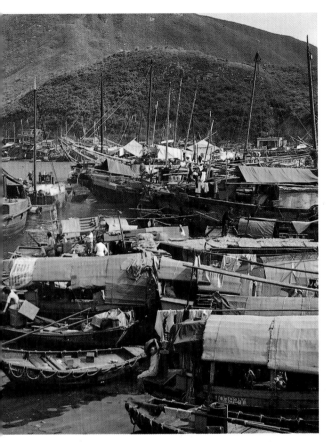

Heaven (or Goddess of the Sea) protectress of fisherfolk, and was built in 1851 on what was then the water's edge. The frieze of pottery figures on the roof is charming. There are two large cast-metal bells on either side of the entrance, one dated 1726 and said to have been found in the sea, and the other dated 1851. The Goddess takes centre stage on the altar, flanked by two life-size military generals, one who can hear clearly and one who can see clearly for one thousand *li* – about 300 miles (480km). But perhaps the most popular shrine in Aberdeen, frequented daily by fishing women burning incense and little paper boats, lies a little to the east of the bus terminal on the waterfront. It comprises several smoke-blackened shrines at the base of an old tree.

On the island of **Ap Lei Chau** ('duck's tongue') on the other side of Aberdeen harbour, traditional boat building techniques are still used in the dockyards. Ap Lei Chau can be reached by a linking bridge, built in 1979, or by shuttle ferry. Aberdeen is world famous for its gigantic floating restaurants. Shuttle services to three restaurants – Jumbo, Sea Palace and Tai Pak – operate from Aberdeen Main Pier or from Shum Wan Ferry Pier (bus no 90 or 97 from the Central Bus Station at Exchange Square).

Repulse Bay Temple is a colourful feature

DEEP WATER BAY AND REPULSE BAY

The scenery on the southern side of the island is quietly spectacular and the beaches of Deep Water Bay and Repulse Bay are usually crowded during the summer bathing season (April to October) with swimmers and barbecue parties. Repulse Bay is called in Chinese 'Shallow Water Bay', which is a true geographical description of this pretty bay, named after HMS *Repulse*, which pursued local pirates. The colonial-style Repulse Bay Hotel once overlooked the bay, but this was unfortunately pulled down in the redevelopment frenzy. So

popular was its elegant veranda restaurant that a replica has been constructed. It is a delightful place to take afternoon tea. British troops occupied the hotel in the face of the Japanese advance around the island and engaged them in battle within the walls of the old hotel – one of the classic incidents in the fall of the island in 1941. The British commander later recalled the event: 'We rolled ... grenades along the beautifully carpeted corridor for all the world as if we'd been in a bowling alley.'

OCEAN PARK/MIDDLE KINGDOM/WATER WORLD

Ocean Park covers 170 hillside acres (69 hectares) with gardens, a huge aviary, a butterfly house, coral atoll, seal and penguin wave cove, shark aquarium, Ocean Park Tower, and funfair rides. Ocean Theatre features daily shows with dolphins, killer whales and high divers. There is also the world's longest outdoor escalator and a cable car ride to the headland.

Middle Kingdom, adjacent, recreates 5,000 years of Chinese history through craft demonstrations, theatre and sideshows.

Open (Ocean Park and Middle Kingdom): daily 10.00–18.00. Separate admission.

Water World, next door to Ocean Park (separate admission) has exciting, water rides plus facilities for swimming.

Open: June to mid-September, daily 10.00–18.00 (21.00 mid-summer).

Ocean Park Citybus: half-hourly from 09.30, from Admiralty MTR station.

STANLEY ✓

Stanley lies on the south side of the island, about 10 minutes by road beyond Repulse Bay. It is one of the island's oldest settlements; when the British came in 1841 the population was around 2,000, and it was one of the first British military bases to be established on Hong Kong Island. At the fall of Hong Kong the men of the Middlesex and Royal Rifles Regiments made a heroic stand against the Japanese, side by side with Volunteer gunners at horrible cost. A brutal civilian internment camp was established at the Stanley Prison by the Japanese and the small military cemetery, dating from the 1840s, is a grim reminder of that suffering. The British Military still occupies part of the Stanley peninsula but this is a restricted area.

Most visitors come here to bargain hunt for designer sportswear, jeans, silk garments and knick-knacks in the shops and stalls of **Stanley Market**. Just walk down Stanley Market Street from the bus stop and you cannot miss it. There are also two good swimming beaches **Stanley Main Beach** and **St Stephen's Beach**.

At the end of Stanley Main Street stands the 18th-century **Tin Hau Temple**, one of the oldest temples on Hong Kong Island, dating from 1767. Inside the temple, dedicated to the Queen of Heaven (or Goddess of the Sea), stands a bell and drum which belonged to the pirate Chang Po Chai, who signalled his ships with them. A

HONG KONG ISLAND – SOUTH

A view of Stanley, lying on the south side of the island

rather tatty tiger's skin hangs on one of the walls, shot near the temple by a Japanese soldier during the occupation. (The poor animal had escaped from a travelling show, so it hardly ranks as a trophy). A forbidding array of black and gold temple gods stands on a stone ledge which runs around three sides of the temple. Tin Hau herself is richly arrayed and the altar reverently curtained. During late April and early May, the Temple comes alive for the Tin Hau Festival.

(Bus no 6 and 260 from Central Bus Station at Exchange Square, go to Repulse Bay and Stanley: a journey of about 45 minutes).

The beach at **Shek O**, around the eastern side of Hong Kong Island, is also popular during the weekends.

KOWLOON

In 1860 the tip of Kowloon peninsula, 4.6 square miles (12 sq km), was ceded to Britain in a very unorthodox fashion. The British negotiators gave a handful of earth wrapped in paper to the Chinese mandarin officials. They in turn handed it back, signifying cession. The area then comprised 10 villages with a population of about 5,000. In 1898 a lease of 99 years on an extra 380 square miles (984 sq km) was agreed upon, which included the New Territories. The name Kowloon means 'Nine Dragons', after the nine peaks which range behind it. In the 13th century the last of the southern Sung Dynasty emperors, a boy-emperor, found a happy refuge here briefly before being drowned off the coast of Lantau Island shortly after. It is said that the young emperor was only able to count eight Dragon peaks and a courtier retorted that the boy himself, a descendant of the Dragon throne, was the ninth. Most of the hills have now disappeared and those that are left are starkly denuded; this deforestation was carried out during the Japanese occupation. The possession of Kowloon peninsula was important, as it secured the Victoria Harbour anchorage from attack by Imperial Chinese batteries. The British built a number of barracks and moved their soldiers from earlier military settlements on Hong Kong Island.

At first the expatriates built holiday homes in Kowloon and it was not until the turn of the century that development took a serious turn. One of the first communities to establish residence here was that of the Portuguese, who built their own Catholic Rosary Church on Chatham Road in 1905. Later they moved to Kowloon Tong which even today is the only true 'suburban' district in Hong Kong. The districts of San Po Kong, Kwun Tong and Kowloon Bay are principally industrial. On multi-storeyed factory premises, silk garments, electronics, cotton cloth, toys, watches, etc, are manufactured for export markets.

WHAT TO SEE

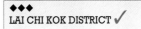

◆◆◆
LAI CHI KOK DISTRICT ✓

The **Sung Dynasty Village** on Lai King Hill Road is a charming representation of life in China during one of its richest periods (AD960–1279). Skilled wood-carvers were brought from China to re-create the architecture while traditionally costumed 'villagers' add to the atmosphere. Visitors to the 60,000 sq ft (5,600 sq m) village are shown a traditional wedding ceremony, acrobatics, and martial arts demonstrations. Calligraphers wield their hair brushes and skilled craftsmen show how to roll incense sticks, make rice paper, and flour noodles.
The Sung Dynasty Village is organised around daily group tours but it is open to individuals between 10.00 and 20.30 (bus no 6A from Kowloon Star Ferry to the last bus stop). Adjacent is **Lai Chi Kok Amusement Park**, a traditional fun-fair park and

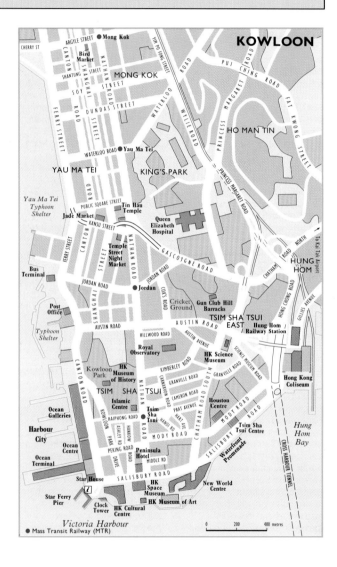

KOWLOON

CHERRY ST

ARGYLE STREET ● Mong Kok

Bird Market

MONG KOK

SHANTUNG STREET

SOY STREET

DUNDAS STREET

CANTON ROAD

NATHAN ROAD

SHANGHAI STREET

FERRY STREET

WATERLOO ROAD

WELL ROAD

TIM PO LONG STREET

PUI CHING ROAD

PRINCESS MARGARET ROAD

FAT KWONG STREET

HO MAN TIN

WATERLOO ROAD ● Yau Ma Tei

YAU MA TEI

KING'S PARK

PRINCESS MARGARET ROAD

Yau Ma Tei Typhoon Shelter

PUBLIC SQUARE STREET

Tin Hau Temple

Jade Market

KANSU STREET

Queen Elizabeth Hospital

GASCOIGNE ROAD

CHATHAM ROAD NORTH

To Kai Tak Airport

HUNG HOM

Temple Street Night Market

JORDAN ROAD

Bus Terminal

FERRY STREET

SHANGHAI STREET

NATHAN ROAD

JORDAN ROAD ● Jordan

COX'S ROAD

Cricket Ground

Gun Club Hill Barracks

HUNG CHONG ROAD

GULEES AVENUE

Post Office

Typhoon Shelter

AUSTIN ROAD

AUSTIN ROAD

TSIM SHA TSUI EAST

Hung Hom Railway Station

HILLWOOD ROAD

AUSTIN AVENUE

Royal Observatory

HK Science Museum

SCIENCE MUSEUM ROAD

Hong Kong Coliseum

Kowloon Park

KIMBERLEY ROAD

HK Museum of History

CANTON ROAD

CARNARVON ROAD

GRANVILLE ROAD

GRANVILLE ROAD SOUTH

TSIM SHA TSUI

NATHAN ROAD

CAMERON ROAD

Houston Centre

MODY ROAD

Ocean Galleries

Islamic Centre

Tsim Sha Tsui ●

PRAT AVENUE

Tsim Sha Tsui Centre

HAIPHONG ROAD

HANKOW ROAD

HANOI RD

MART. AVE

Hung Hom Bay

Harbour City

KOWLOON PARK DRIVE

ASHLEY RD

MODY ROAD

CHATHAM ROAD SOUTH

Ocean Centre

PEKING ROAD

MIDDLE RD

Peninsula Hotel

SALISBURY ROAD

Waterfront Promenade

CROSS HARBOUR TUNNEL

Ocean Terminal

Star House

SALISBURY ROAD

New World Centre

Star Ferry Pier

Clock Tower

HK Cultural Centre

HK Space Museum

HK Museum of Art

Victoria Harbour

● Mass Transit Railway (MTR)

0   200   400 metres

Kowloon, or 'Nine Dragons', was named in the 13th century; Sung Dynasty Village recreates that period

a skating rink (open Monday to Friday 12.00–21.30; Saturday 11.00–22.30; Sunday and holidays 10.00–21.30). Admission charge.

Another site in the area is the **Lei Cheng Uk Museum**, 41 Tonkin Street, Sham Shui Po. The Han Dynasty burial vault (AD25–220) was discovered in 1955 during site work for a government housing estate. The tomb itself (four brick chambers in the form of a cross) and tomb objects are on display (open daily, except Thursday, 10.00–13.00 and 14.00–18.00; Sundays and public holidays 13.00–18.00). Admission free.

◆◆
LEI YUE MUN

At the edge of Kowloon, Lei Yue Mun is a fishing village noted for its seaside restaurants. The seafood vendors keep their live produce in gurgling tanks and vats, and each evening the main village alley livens up as Cantonese seafood gourmets descend, often from pleasure craft. They bargain fiercely, then carry their purchases off to a nearby restaurant to be cooked. Be warned, though, that this is not a cheap way to dine.

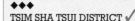

◆◆◆
TSIM SHA TSUI DISTRICT ✓

Tsim Sha Tsui, meaning Sharp, Sandy Point, is the heart of Kowloon's commercial and tourist district. Its shopping centres, hotels and restaurants are a visitors' mecca. The main tree-lined thoroughfare is **Nathan Road**, running for 3 miles (5km) in a north-south axis. When constructed at the turn of the century it was called Nathan's Folly, after Governor Sir Matthew Nathan (1904–1907), whose pet project it was. It was seen as both unnecessary and an extravagance. Now the Tsim Sha Tsui section is known more affectionately as 'the Golden Mile'. Off Nathan Road runs a web of streets, ablaze with shop signs in Chinese and English, which offer just about everything a person could wish for. Major shopping complexes include **Harbour City**, on the waterfront beside the Kowloon Star Ferry Pier. This incorporates Ocean Centre, Ocean Terminal and Ocean Galleries to create a huge shopping and hotel area

Shop signs vie for attention in the tourist area of Tsim Sha Tsui

along Canton Road. The New World Centre on Salisbury Road is another example of an up-market shopping paradise. The **Hong Kong Museum of History**, within Kowloon Park, concentrates on local history, with changing exhibitions on subjects such as traditional village life, fishing craft and archaeology. (Open daily, except Friday, 10.00–18.00; Sunday and public holidays 13.00–18.00; admission HK$10).

By the Star Ferry concourse stands a **Clock Tower** which has been preserved as a monument to the old Kowloon–Canton Railway station built in 1916. The old station stood on this site until 1975 and travellers could board a train here and journey all the way to Europe, through China, Mongolia and Russia. Now it is the site of the **Hong Kong Cultural Centre**, which since its completion in 1989, has been much criticised for its modernistic style. Under its innovative 'ski-slope' roof lies a 2,100-seat concert hall, 1,750-seat grand theatre, and a smaller studio theatre. The Cultural Centre complex houses the **Hong Kong Museum of Art** with its impressive collection of Chinese paintings, ceramics, bronzes, jade and embroideries. A separate gallery displays the Xubaizhai collection of Chinese painting and calligraphy. (Open daily, except Thursday, 10.00–18.00; Sunday and public holidays 13.00–18.00).

Also part of the Cultural Centre complex is the **Hong Kong Space Museum** with one of the world's largest and most sophisticated planetariums. Wide-screen

Omnimax films and sky shows are presented in the Space Theatre. In addition, the Hall of Space Science and Hall of Astronomy explain recent developments in space astronomy. (Open daily, except Tuesday, 13.00–21.00; Saturday, Sunday and public holidays 10.00–21.00. Under three's not admitted. Admission charge. For show times, tel: 2734 9009).

Another major tourist area is **Tsim Sha Tsui East**. Developed on the site of the old marshalling yards of the Kowloon–Canton Railway. Today there are many major hotels – Grand Stanford Crowne Plaza Harbour View, Kowloon Shangri-La, Nikko, Regal Kowloon, Royal Garden – plus restaurants and shopping malls. A major new attraction is the **Hong Kong Science Museum**, on Science Museum Road. Here the mysteries of science are unravelled by way of 500 exhibits (mostly 'hands-on'), plus a fascinating robotics display. (Open daily, except Monday, 13.00–21.00; Saturday, Sunday and public holidays 10.00–21.00).

A walk along the **Waterfront Promenade** between Kowloon Star Ferry Pier and Tsim Sha Tsui East, presents a grand vista of Victoria Harbour with its yachts, tugs, junks, pleasure launches and visiting warships.

Another landmark is the **Peninsula Hotel** on Salisbury Road. Built in 1925 (with the central extension completed in 1995) in grand colonial style to cater for international travellers, it found its spacious rooms occupied by troops after the government requisitioned the hotel during the crisis year of 1925, when Hong

Kong had a general strike and boycott of British goods. Hong Kong's Chinese workers supported their compatriots in the foreign concessions of Shanghai and Canton where labour demonstrations had taken an anti-foreign turn and ended in machine-gun massacres. Officially opened in 1928, the hotel went into business only to be requisitioned by Japanese officers during the occupation: the British formally surrendered in front of the hotel in 1941.

The distinctive Islamic architecture of **Jamia Masjid Mosque** – on the corner of Nathan and Haiphong Road may seem oddly incongruous in Hong Kong, but there are over 50,000 Muslims in the territory, most of them Chinese. Islam was introduced to China around the 7th century by Arab traders. To visit the mosque tel: 2724 0095.

WONG TAI SIN DISTRICT
The large modern **Wong Tai Sin Temple** is on Lung Cheung Road and was built in the 1970s. Wong Tai Sin is said to have been a young shepherd when he was taken by an immortal and taught how to make an elixir of immortality. Today his followers believe that he is able to cure illnesses as well as bestowing luck at the races.

Alongside the temple are fortune tellers' stalls displaying their physiognomy and palmistry charts. The physiognomists work from classical reference books which were first written in the Sung (AD960–1279) and Ch'ing (AD1644–1912) Dynasties,

although the art is mentioned in histories of the 2nd century BC (open daily 07.00–17.00). Donations.
MTR Subway: Wong Tai Sin.

YAU MA TEI & MONG KOK DISTRICTS
One of the many curious sights in Hong Kong is the **Bird Market** on Hong Lok Street (Mong Kok MTR

Wong Tai Sin Temple is dedicated to a god only introduced to Hong Kong as recently as 1915

Canton Road and **Shanghai Street**, west of Jordan Road, both present an absorbing array of items on sale in their shops: sequined Chinese wedding dresses, bamboo steamers, gold ornaments, mahjong sets, snakes, fragrant incense and temple ware.

Jade Market is found under the Gascoigne Road flyover on Kansu Street, Yau Ma Tei (take MTR to Jordan station). The dealers display trays of carved jade pendants, rings, bracelets and ornaments. But unless you know something about jade, just buy for pleasure and enjoy bargaining. Serious Chinese buyers can be seen negotiating secret deals using sign language. A translucent green jade bracelet is traditionally bought by Chinese women to celebrate the birth of a son. Chinese hold jade in the highest esteem and Confucius wrote: 'It is soft, smooth and shining like kindness; it is hard, fine and strong, like intelligence; its edges seem sharp, but do not cut, like justice; it hangs down to the ground like humility; when struck, it gives a clear, ringing sound, like music; the stains in it which are not hidden and add to its beauty are like truthfulness; its brightness is like heaven, while its firm substance, born of mountains and the water, is like the earth.'

The market is open from 10.00 to 15.30 daily.

Temple Street Night Market, Temple Street, Yau Ma Tei, comes to life each night between 18.00 and 23.00. This colourful and lively market sells cheap clothing, with the emphasis on mens' wear. Its food stalls,

station). Chinese greatly prize singing birds, and pay high prices for a good songster. Finely crafted bird cages and delicate little porcelain feeding bowls can also demand high prices. There are hundreds of imported birds on sale each day from 10.00 to 18.00.

KOWLOON

story tellers and fortune tellers reading palms and faces, make this an interesting night excursion.

Tin Hau Temple near Public Square Street (close to the Jade Market) in Yau Ma Tei, although dedicated to the Queen of Heaven (or Goddess of the Sea), has a number of other deities under the same roof. In its four halls are statues of the City God, God of Earth, the Goddess of Mercy and the God of Justice. Worshippers at the temple, built about 120 years ago, were mostly boat people from the nearby typhoon shelter (see below). Red-robed Taoist monks officiate at special services and the temple is always busy with devout believers. The wall of one

of the halls is lined with 60 gods, wrapped in red paper – one for each year of the Chinese 60-year cycle (open daily 08.00–18.00).

Yau Ma Tei Typhoon Shelter on Ferry Street (Yau Ma Tei MTR station) was home to many Hoklo and Tanka boat people whose traditional fishing grounds were the south China coast. They spoke different dialects and practised their own customs. Today the boat people have been rehoused in new estates. Along the waterfront a procession of lighters and junks load and unload their cargoes.

In the streets behind Ferry Street, lying south of Waterloo Road, there are wood-carvers' shops making decorated Chinese deities, as well as mahjong houses.

A fine way to see the sights

NEW TERRITORIES

Until some 20 years ago the New Territories, leased to Britain in 1898 for 99 years, were still mainly agricultural, the villagers leading a traditional rural lifestyle growing crops of vegetables and rice. Very few pockets of this old society exist today, and less rice is grown. The paddy fields lie fallow and overgrown, simply awaiting an offer from a suitable real estate developer. Many of the older villagers live on remittances from relatives living and working overseas, and spend their time in tea houses gossiping and playing *mahjong*. The rapid development of vast high rise towns has completely changed the nature of the area, and vast roadworks are underway to deal with the ever-growing cross-border traffic with China. The electrification of the Kowloon–Canton Railway (KCR) has put the New Territories into the commuter belt. One-third of Hong Kong's population has been rehoused here. The land was settled by five main Chinese clans, who are Cantonese speaking and known as Punti or 'locals'. Their clan connections lay in nearby Guangdong province, and they began arriving between the 12th and 14th centuries, settling first in the rich flats in the northwest of the New Territories around Tuen Mun, Yuen Long, San Tin and Sheung Shui. The Hakka (which means 'guest' or 'tenant') came to the area only in the 17th century, settling in the eastern part of the New Territories and speaking their own dialect. The Hakka women wear distinctive round straw hats hung with a black frill and are frequently seen working on construction sites.

During the mid 17th century the south China coast was infested with pirates who terrorised the inhabitants. Emperor Kang Hsi ordered a coastal evacuation of all villages in 1661, so as to deny supplies and information to the pirates. The clans suffered enormously as a result and when they were eventually allowed back to their lands a decade later, they were much depleted in numbers. They took on the Hakkas as tenant farmers.

When the British leased the New Territories there were about 700 extant villages. A village was sited according to the geomantic principles of *fung shui* (wind and rain), which usually meant building houses close together at the foot of a hill and just above the paddy fields, cramming them into parallel terraces with narrow access lanes. Trees were planted to deflect negative *fung shui* influences and protect the village. Even with such enormous consideration given to the siting of a village there could be problems. At Sun Uk Village, for instance, the first position was found to be very propitious for accumulating wealth but not for the birth of male children. The demand for male progeny outweighed all other needs, and the clan moved to another site. Boundaries of villages were also often set according to *fung shui* needs and this caused inter-village strife.

Clans built ancestral halls in their villages in accordance with the Confucian ethics of filial piety and ancestral worship, and these are still used at special clan celebrations. The tablets of the ancestors are kept here (immediate ancestors are also worshipped at small family altars in the house). Some clan halls have recently been restored. You can explore the New Territories by taking the Kowloon–Canton Railway (KCR) from Kowloon railway station and getting off at any of the stations (except Lo Wu); or explore on the local buses, or take a six-hour 'Land Between' tour, organised by the Hong Kong Tourist Association for HK$295 (adult), HK$245 (child/senior). For more information tel: 2801 7111.

WHAT TO SEE

♦♦♦
CASTLE PEAK ✓

The sheltered Castle Peak Bay was used in the 11th century as a lay-by port for all manner of trading boats from the Indian Ocean and the Middle East. Here boats converged, awaiting the arrival of monsoon winds to assist their passage to Canton. The bay gradually silted up and is just a swimming beach today.

Castle Peak Monastery
overlooks Tuen Mun New Town and Castle Peak Bay from the slope of 1,913-ft (583m) high Ching Shan (Green Mountain, as it is called in Chinese, but Castle Peak in English). It is believed to have been established more than 1,500 years ago by a roving Buddhist monk called Pui To, who, it is said, could cross rivers in a wooden bowl. There are many other extraordinary tales about the monastery's founder.

Junks come to rest in the tranquil Castle Peak Bay

The monastery must have been quite important to Chinese seamen whose boats used to gather in the bay, but the present buildings date from the 1920s only. The terraced halls of the monastery are surrounded by pine trees, fruit trees and gardens, and the graves of its monks and nuns over the ages. Three large gold leaf, wooden statues – the Buddhas of the Past, Present and Future – stand

encased in the main hall. A small stone statue of the Founder stands in a cave alcove above the monastery, where he is said to have spent time in meditation. It is thought that the statue may have been carved as early as AD954.

Although it is a Buddhist establishment, the architecture and some of the statuary are Taoist additions, for during most of the 19th century it was, in fact, a Taoist temple. A small vegetarian restaurant serves visitors and devotees. The monastery is the oldest in the territory.

Ching Chung Koon (Green Pine) Temple on Ching Koon Road, Tuen Mun is dedicated to one of the Taoist Eight Immortals of Chinese mythology, Lu Sun Young, expeller of evil. He fulfils his task with the aid of a magical fly-switch and sword. The temple is a centre of Taoist studies with a very valuable library of almost 4,000 volumes and some fine works of art. A 1,000-year-old jade seal, imperial palace lanterns and antique porcelain adorn the halls.

The buildings themselves are not old – dating from 1949 – but the hall interiors are ornate and traditional.

Apart from scholarly pursuits, the temple supports an old people's home within the complex. It is popular among locals, who visit the temple and large garden, and eat at its vegetarian restaurant.

Beside Lam Tei Light Rail Transit Station, two spectacular dragons guard the entrance to **Miu Fat Monastery**, regarded as one of the greatest temples in south-east Asia. The interior is adorned with more than 10,000 Buddha sculptures and Chinese and Thai paintings.

◆◆
FANLING

The morning (10.30 to 12 noon) **Luen Wo Market**, off Sha Tau Kok Road at Fanling (established in 1948), is a typical New Territories market place, where arithmetic is done on an abacus and the smells of beancurd, ginger, garlic and fish pervade.

There are two fine old walled villages around Fanling: **San Wai** was settled by the Tang Clan about 250 years ago and some 30-odd families live in the village, some still bearing the Tang name. The dry moat still exists but all that remains of the walls is the main gate tower with a superb old iron lattice gate.

The walled village of **Hakka Wai** is a beautiful example of Chinese village architecture. It was built in 1905 by the Wong family and the villagers are very proud of it. Terracotta frogs and fishes decorate the roof drains and a

three-storey watch tower stands at one end of the village.

◆◆
SAI KUNG PENINSULA

This area of the New Territories is the most beautiful and certainly, to date, least developed region, with lovely mountains, valleys, old villages and stretches of beach. Marinas and yacht clubs are a feature of Hebe Haven, and there are waterfront restaurants specialising in Hakka cuisine, and an old market place at Sai Kung town.

Several temples and shrines in Sai Kung are dedicated to Tin Hau, Queen of Heaven (or Goddess of the Sea) and to Koon Yum, Goddess of Mercy, and annual festivals are big events for the fishing communities in Port Shelter and Rocky Harbour.

The tiny agricultural village of **Sheung Yiu**, has been converted to what is now the **Sheung Yiu Folk Museum** with exhibits of farm tools, cooking utensils and household furnishing (open daily, except Tuesday, 09.00–16.00). Admission free.

◆◆◆
SHA TIN

During the Ch'ing Dynasty (AD1644–1912), rice grown in quiet Sha Tin valley was so excellent that it was reserved for the emperor alone. The inlet and gentle green valley gave a peaceful picture even in the early 1970s. Today it is a modern city with a projected population of 700,000 by the end of the century! **Amah Rock**, on top of the mountain range, above Sha Tin, watches over these giant changes. The rock, in the shape of a woman carrying a child on her back, has a moving legend attached to it. It is said that the woman is the wife of a bodyguard of the last Sung boy-emperor, who was killed in battle. Each evening she would carry her child to the peak and wait in vain for her husband. Eventually the gods took pity on her loyal patience and turned her body to stone while releasing her soul to be united with her husband.

Che Kung Temple, Che Kung Miu Road, is dedicated to a Sung Dynasty (AD960–1279) general, whose military exploits earned deification after his death. The

Hong Kong is not all skyscrapers: this Chinese Village is in Sha Tin

temple was erected, around 1825, in his honour after a villager dreamt that the god had stopped a deadly plague which ravaged the village towards the end of the Ming Dynasty. On the third day of each lunar New Year the Che Kung festival draws tens of thousands of worshippers. On the altar is a wheel which symbolises the cosmic rotation of the year. Devotees turn this to bring good luck for the new year and present their offerings. Che Kung is especially popular amongst gamblers! Che Kung Temple is a 15-minute walk from the KCR Tai Wai station.

The **Chinese University** campus near Tai Po Road at Sha Tin was established in 1963 and courses are taught principally in Chinese, although English is also a teaching medium. Competition is very keen for the 10,000 or so places. An extra-mural department has an enrolment of some 43,000 students.

The University has its own **art gallery** in which exhibitions are held regularly. The University's own collection of art includes ancient bronze seals, jade flower carvings, paintings and calligraphy (open daily, 10.00–16.30; Sunday and some public holidays 12.30–16.30). To obtain information on the most current exhibition themes tel: 2609 7416.

KCR: University station.

Tao Fong Shan is a hill to the northwest of Sha Tin where the Chinese Mission to Buddhists has stood since 1931. The founder was Karl Ludvig Reichelt, whose life was dedicated to teaching Christianity to Buddhists. The buildings integrate Buddhist

A golden Buddha dwarfs the ranks of 12,800 tiny statues in Ten Thousand Buddhas Monastery

architectural principles and the gardens are wonderfully peaceful. Former monks are engaged in painting pottery to contribute to the mission. (About half an hour's walk from KCR Sha Tin station.)

More than four hundred steps lead to the hilltop **Ten Thousand Buddhas Monastery (Man Fat**

miraculous body was lacquered and encased in gold leaf and, before a congregation of 10,000 Buddhists, was enthroned at the foot of the huge 40-ft (12m) high Buddha in the temple. A climb to the top of the pink pagoda affords a panoramic view of Sha Tin below. (Half an hour's walk from KCR Sha Tin station.)

Sha Tin Race Course was opened in 1978 and stands on 250 acres (101 hectares) of reclaimed land. Its facilities, which includes air-conditioned stables, are among the most modern in the world, and its spectator stands accommodate 83,000 racing enthusiasts (see **Sporting Activities**, page 109). KCR Race Course station.

Tsang Tai Uk (Tsang's Big House), near Tai Chung Kui Road and Sha Kok Street, was built as the Tsang clan family residence in the 1840s. It has a high rectangular defensive wall and corner towers with *wok-yee* (meaning 'ear of a cooking pan') roofs. Atop each corner tower is a trident to ward off evil. The dwellings within face on to a central courtyard. One local legend says that the family's prosperity was due to the visitation of pirates, who left several large jars of fish in the safe-keeping of the Tsang clan headman. When the pirates failed to return, the fish were thrown away and, behold, the pots were full of silver coins.

The Tsangs then decided to build their fortified village to defend themselves against the return of the pirates. Many of the houses are rented out and only a few members of the Tsang family reside there now. (Tsang Tai Uk

Tze), built in 1950. The walls of the main hall are lined with 12,800 tiny statues and three large gilded ones of the Lord Buddha. Three other small temples make up the complex, one of which has the embalmed body of the founder monk, Yuet Kai, who died in 1965 at the grand old age of 87. It is said that his body was found to be in perfect condition when, following the monks' instructions, it was exhumed eight months later. The

Hong Kong's second race course, at Sha Tin, took seven years to build

is a 5 to 10 minute ride from the KCR Sha Tin station.)

◆
SHEUNG SHUI

Sheung Shui is the last stop on the Kowloon-Canton Railway if you are not bound for China. Hakka women with their distinctive black fringed hats are frequent shoppers in the covered market in the centre of the old section of town. The market played a vital role in Sheung Shui; regular market days were the economic focus of the town until the 1940s. Sheung Shui is part of the Fanling new town conurbation with a planned 250,000 population. From **Lok Ma Chau Lookout Point** the view sweeps across duck and fish ponds to beyond the Hong Kong/China border river of Shenzen into mainland China. A major border crossing point is under construction close by.

◆◆
TAI PO

The old Tai Po market town has been transformed by massive reclamation along the seashore of Tolo Harbour where residential blocks and an industrial estate have been constructed. Tai Po's market is still of interest, as is the white colonial-style bungalow known as **Island House**, in Tuen

Chau Tsai, on Tai Po Road, now occupied by the World Wide Fund for Nature (Hong Kong) but formerly the home of successive Tai Po district officers. Island House was used as the Japanese command headquarters for the New Territories during World War II.

The old railway station building at Tai Po has been turned into the **Hong Kong Railway Museum** with old carriages and memorabilia of its heyday (open daily, except Tuesday, 09.00–16.00). Admission free. From Ma Lui Shui pier a ferry leaves twice a day on a four-hour round trip to islands in Tolo Harbour. As early as the 8th century, historical records mention pearl diving in Tolo Harbour by Tanka people as corvée labour. Divers were weighted down with stones and were pulled to the surface by a rope when on the point of drowning. Surprisingly, the Mongol Yuan Dynasty considered it inhumane and in the 14th century prohibited the industry. But it seems to have resumed again in the Ming Dynasty (AD1368–1644). For information on this trip contact the Hong Kong Tourist Association (see **Tourist Offices**, page 123). **Kadoorie Experimental Farm**, on Lam Kam Road to the west of Tai Po along the Lam Tsuen Valley (bus no 64K from Tai Po KCR station), is a beautiful garden of trees, shrubs and flowers. It forms part of a 360-acre (146-hectare) farm run by the two Kadoorie brothers, well known Hong Kong philanthropists. Since 1949 their Agricultural Aid Association has given aid and

know-how in agricultural and animal husbandry, built roads and bridges, and helped more than 1,200 villages in the territory. A re-training programme has also been established for Gurkha soldiers returning to their villages in Nepal. Visits to the farm can be arranged – they are by appointment only (tel: 2488 1317). On the north side of Tolo Harbour lies Plover Cove Reservoir, above which is the beautiful Pak Sin Range, offering hard but rewarding walks. The road leads on towards Starling Inlet via **Bride's Pool Waterfalls**, where two small waterfalls make a popular picnic spot.

At **Luk Keng** an egretry has been established for the small egrets which nest here during the summer months. The low mangroves and still water make ideal fishing grounds for the birds. As many as 800 nests have been counted among the forest of trees on the small hill. The road links up with the Sha Tau Kok Road. The town of Sha Tau Kok (within the closed border area) can be seen across the inlet. This town has been transformed in recent years from a tiny border village to an important border crossing town.

TSUEN WAN

The **Sam Tung Uk Museum** is a mid-18th century Hakka walled village which belonged to the Chan clan. It has survived the growth of the industrial satellite town of Tsuen Wan and has been landscaped, restored and converted to a delightful folk museum, with permanent

NEW TERRITORIES

exhibitions of farming implements and furniture (open daily, except Tuesdays and some public holidays, 09.00–16.00). Admission free.

MTR subway: Tsuen Wan station.

♦♦♦
YUEN LONG ✓

Concentrated urbanisation has taken place in Yuen Long, with major public and private housing projects. This once sleepy market town now has a population of around 133,000 and by the end of the century this should reach 140,000. Yuen Long is linked to Tuen Mun by a light rail system (LRT).

East of Yuen Long lie the 500-year-old walled villages of the Tang clan, the most accessible being **Kat Hing Wai**, a walled village on Kam Tin Road. The walls and corner towers were built to defend villages against pirate incursion and the rich Tang clan were obvious targets. In 1898 the British army took retribution against the Tang, who were militant towards the British takeover of the New Territories, by removing their handsome iron gates. After adorning an Irish garden for 26 years the gates were returned to the village in 1925. This is the most commercialised of the New Territories villages and is geared for tourists. A donation is expected.

Lau Fau Shan, a fishing village to the west of Yuen Long, is famous for its seafood restaurants. The narrow main street is lined with vendors selling live and dried seafood specialities. You may buy what you fancy and take it to any restaurant in the village for cooking. The morning fish market, which supplies fish and shellfish to most of the New Territories and Kowloon restaurants, is very lively and competitive. Most of the villagers make their living from oyster beds in Deep Bay, but recently these have suffered from pollution. Oyster shells bank the shorefront.

Ha Tsuen village, near by, built by the Tang clan, has a fine 18th-century ancestral hall. Inside its grey brick walls are two courtyards, and the main hall has two wooden tablets with the characters for brotherly love and filial piety. The ancestral tablets are arranged on an ornately carved altar. Just inside the entrance is a 'spirit wall' which traditionally prevents ghosts and evil spirits from entering the hall.

A 19th-century Chinese cannon, unearthed near the village in 1979, stands at the doorway. Outside **Ping Shan** village stands an elegant three-storey brick pagoda dating from the 14th century, the Tsui Shing Lau. The pagoda is said to have

For those who think of Hong Kong as crowds and skyscrapers, areas such as these New Territories fields can be a revelation

A pied kingfisher – one of the hundreds of species of birds to be seen at Mai Po Marshes

originally had seven storeys, but these appear to have been lost in typhoons. It is simple and graceful and is also the only old one left in the territory.

Mai Po Marshes Bird Sanctuary, on the Hong Kong-Chinese border, off Castle Peak Road, between Lok Ma Chau and Yuen Long, is a designated World Wide Fund for Nature (Hong Kong) wetlands.

Over 250 species of birds have been sighted during the migratory season when Mai Po's ponds, mudflats and mangroves serve as a vital feeding site. Commonly seen are herons, egrets, kingfishers and ibises.

There are well-constructed hides and a boardwalk which gives access to the mangrove swamps. The Chinese Government has also declared 7 miles (11km) of contiguous wetlands a nature reserve, and it is hoped that further developmental encroachment can be contained. For details of visits to Mai Po Marshes see **Peace and Quiet** section (page 63).

San Tin village on Castle Peak Road near the Mai Po Marshes is an extended village founded by the Man clan and has at least five large ancestral halls. The oldest, built in the late 17th century, has three halls with decorated and carved wooden roof supports and stone columns. Although it has not been restored recently it is still in reasonable, if dusty, condition. The newest hall was built in 1972 and is an interesting contrast in style and taste. In 1865 a successful Man clan member who achieved high honours in the Imperial Civil Service examinations in Peking, built himself a grand two-storey family residence in grey brick, known as **Tai Fu Tai**. The house has recently been beautifully restored with financial assistance from the Hong Kong Jockey Club. Its wooden carvings and wall paintings have been repaired and repainted, and ancestral portraits hung above the altar. The tiled roof is adorned with brightly glazed terracotta figures and a large side-kitchen shows a series of cooking stoves. Behind the house is a grove of old *lichee* (lychee) trees (open daily, except Tuesday, 09.00–13.00 and 14.00–17.00).

OUTLYING ISLANDS

There are 235 islands in Hong Kong waters. Most of them are barren rocks with no water supply and therefore uninhabitable; others have small fishing communities. A ferry ride and half-day or day's exploration of one or more of these islands is an opportunity to enjoy the slower pace of village life, or to walk their peaceful hills for stunning sea views.
Ferries for the main islands leave from the Outlying Districts Services Pier, west of the Star Ferry Pier on Hong Kong Island.

About ten per cent of Cheung Chau's population lives in the 'junk villages' off the island's shores

Check the ferry schedule either with the Hong Kong Ferry (Holdings) Company (tel: 2542 3082) or with the Hong Kong Tourist Association (tel: 2807 6177). It is preferable to go on a weekday, as the weekend ferries are packed with young holiday-makers. Ferry fares range from HK$8 to HK$26.50. Detailed maps of the islands can be purchased at the Government Publications Centre, General Post Office Building, beside the Hong Kong Star Ferry concourse.

CHEUNG CHAU

The small island of Cheung Chau, an hour's ferry ride from Central, has become a commuter island, as rents are

OUTLYING ISLANDS

Beaches and an absence of traffic draw visitors to Cheung Chau

low and the ferry service frequent (last one back leaves at 22.30; also by hovercraft, weekdays only). The population is about 40,000 but it retains much character with a busy market and harbour, temples, beaches and scenic walks. Cars are not allowed on the island. A hundred years ago Cheung Chau was the home of a pirate fleet of over 250 junks. On the southern tip of the island is the **Cheung Po Tsai Cave**, named after their commander. Even as recently as the 1920s, pirates would harass passing boats. There are a number of temples on the island, but the most important is **Pak Tai Temple**, in whose harbour the spectacular Bun Festival is held each April/May. On the east side of

the island, along Hak Pak Road rock carvings depicting animal shapes which may have been carved two or three thousand years ago. Shops sell paper houses, cars, clothing, etc, for burning at funerals, for Cheung Chau is considered geomantically very auspicious for burials, and there are many cemeteries on the southern part of the island

◆◆
LAMMA
Ferries link the two main villages of **Yung Shue Wan** and **Sok Kwu Wan** on Lamma Island with Central (from Central Harbour Services Pier), and a *kai do* (motorised sampan) service operates between Aberdeen (south Hong Kong Island) and Sok Kwu Wan. The island's population of only 3,000 are either vegetable growers or run fish farms in the bays, but there

are 'city' types, too, who commute every day. Carbon dating of archaeological finds indicates that Lamma was occupied as early as 4000BC. A favourite walk over the hills between the two main villages of Yung Shue Wan and Sok Kwu Wan takes less than two hours.

◆◆◆
LANTAU ✓

Lantau is a beautiful island of mountains, valleys, beaches, peaceful monasteries, and old Chinese forts, which is twice the size of Hong Kong Island but with a population of less than 20,000. It is ideal for walking and there are two designated country parks with well marked hiking paths. At Discovery Bay a large residential scheme offers sporting facilities, including a golf course, and a fast boat service operates from Blake Pier in Central to the bay for commuters and visitors alike. The ferry, which takes just over an hour from the Outlying District Services Pier (Central), and the hovercraft (35 mins) from Government Pier (Central), dock at Mui Wo (Silvermine Bay). Buses leave from the ferry pier for the villages of Tai O and Tung Chung and for Po Lin Monastery. There is a taxi service or minibuses can be arranged beforehand with Lantau Tours Ltd (tel: 2984 8255/6).
Several neolithic and Bronze Age archaeological sites have been excavated on Lantau, indicating that the island was occupied as early as 2500BC. At the end of the 13th century the exiled court of the last Sung Dynasty child

emperor resided for a short time on Lantau.
Cheung Sha is a long sandy beach, the best on the island, just beyond Pui O on the southern coast of the island; and **Mui Wo** (Silvermine Bay) is a small beachfront resort.
Po Lin Monastery (Precious Lotus Monastery) was founded in 1905, and stands on Lantau Peak, 2,460ft (750m) above sea level. Buddhist monks from other parts of southeast Asia gather here every two years for meditation and special initiation ceremonies. The present buildings were built in 1970 and the temple architecture is on a grand scale, with marble terraces and striking yellow roof tiles. It is dedicated to the Three Precious Buddhas – the religion's founder, Lord Sakyamuni, the Healing Buddha, and Lord of the Western Paradise, Amitabha. A vegetarian restaurant serves simple meals to the thousands of weekly visitors and the income from this enterprise and from donations supports the monastery. Standing on a plateau opposite the monastery, and visible from the sea, is one of southeast Asia's tallest outdoor bronze buddha standing at 88ft (26.4m) and weighing 246 tons (250 tonnes) – it was constructed in 1990 at a cost of HK$68 million.
Close by is **Lantau Tea Gardens,** a tea plantation growing *Wan Mo Cha* ('cloud and mist tea'), which can be tasted in their café.
Tai O village has a population of 6,500, who are mostly engaged in catching and drying fish. Dried out salt pans are all that remains of the salt factories which flourished here 200 years

ago. It is a quaint village, with many fishing huts built on stilts along the tidal creek, which is crossed in a rope-drawn sampan (a 30 cent ride). The narrow Market Street leads to the 18th-century **Kwan Tai Temple**, and to the 17th-century **Hau Wong Temple**. A festival is held each year to commemorate Hau Wong, who was the Marquis Yeung, a beloved guardian of the last Sung Dynasty boy-emperor.

Tung Chung village is the site of a Chinese fort built in 1817 by the Viceroy of Kwangtung; its cannon served to repel coastal attacks. It has thick granite stone walls and ramparts which display six Chinese cannon, the earliest

dated 1805. The fort has been restored as a historical monument. On the bluff overlooking the ferry pier and bay are the ruins of the Tung Chung Battery. Local Chinese historical records refer to it as forming a part of the coastal fortification, but the site has not been excavated. The village also has a Hau Wong Temple.

PENG CHAU

Ferries bound for Lantau Island normally stop *en route* at Peng Chau Island. The residents here are mostly engaged in fishing or fish farming, though there are some porcelain factories in operation. The island does not offer much in the way of beaches or pleasant walks, beyond the curiosity of exploration.

The dazzlingly decorated Po Lin Monastery on Lantau Island, founded in 1905

PEACE AND QUIET

Wildlife and Countryside in Hong Kong
by Paul Sterry

Although many of the territory's animals and plants are widespread throughout the mainland of China, Hong Kong provides the easiest opportunities to see them. It is also on an important migration route for birds heading from their Asian breeding grounds to winter in the tropics, and its coastal marshes, in particular, are of international importance. Hong Kong has a wide variety of habitats and its scenery is often dramatic. Beaches, mangroves, marshes and cliffs line undeveloped stretches of the coast and rise inland to hills and mountains nearly 3,000 ft (1,000m) above sea level. In places, woodlands and open grassland cover these heights and upland valleys sometimes also contain reservoirs.
The variety of habitats is reflected in the wealth of plant and animal species found; for example, nearly 400 species of birds have been recorded, over 100 of which breed. Butterflies are diverse and abundant and there are nearly 2,908 species of native and introduced flowering plants and ferns.

Land of Contrasts

First impressions would perhaps lead the visitor to suppose that this is not an area for the wildlife enthusiast. While this may be true of many of the more built up areas, places of tranquil beauty can be found without too much difficulty, with colourful and exotic butterflies and birds. Despite its well-deserved reputation for being overcrowded, Hong Kong's densely-packed urban areas are comparatively restricted and over three-quarters of the 400 or so square miles (1,000 sq km) in the territory can be classed as countryside. While much of the land is in some way influenced by man or his agriculture, 21 country parks, covering an area of 102,104 acres (41,320 hectares) have been established and a further series of nature reserves helps conserve the land and its wildlife. The parks and reserves cover all types of habitat from the coastal beaches and marshes to wooded hills and reservoirs, and in addition to the birds and flowering plants, mammals such as barking deer and civet also benefit from this protection.
On Hong Kong Island itself, the Botanical Gardens in the Central District have been established since 1864 and their quiet corners are attractive to both resident and wintering birds. Elsewhere, there are five country parks and the 30-mile (50km) 'Hong Kong Trail' has been set out to enable the hiker to traverse them all. Particularly interesting is the Aberdeen Country Park, which lies inland from Deep Water Bay, and has extensive woodlands which enclose two reservoirs. Aberdeen Country Park can be reached by following the road inland from Aberdeen. Public transport is also available from Central. There is a visitor centre which provides information about the nature trail and other routes around the wooded reservoirs.

PEACE AND QUIET

At least one of Hong Kong's birds actually seems to benefit from the abundance of people. Black kites, often referred to as blackeared kites, are abundant and thrive on refuse. On an environmental level, sewage and litter, animal waste and industrial emissions are a real problem for the Hong Kong authorities, but fortunately, the problem is now recognised and immediate and long-term plans to curb and monitor pollution are having a real effect.

Boat Trips

In a territory where many of the people live on offshore islands, boats are an essential mode of transport. There are also many sight-seeing trips available and together with the ferries they provide an extremely pleasant way of seeing Hong Kong and visiting the more distant peninsulas and remote islands. Some of the journeys are comparatively short and may simply involve crossing a harbour, while others, such as the ferry to Lantau, are much longer. After a while, long sea journeys can become a little monotonous, so what better way to inject interest than to observe the wildlife?

In shallow bays and unpolluted harbours you may see shoals of fish. The marine life in the South China Sea off Hong Kong is exceedingly rich and diverse and this is especially evident in the numbers of fish. About 1,500 species are found in the inshore waters, coral reefs and open seas around the coast, this wealth being manifested in the extraordinary variety found in the markets of Hong Kong.

Cattle egrets are usually to be found on cultivated land and in marshy areas such as Mai Po

The secret of the diversity of Hong Kong's marine environment lies in its position on the Asian coast. The warm, tropical waters bathing coastlines further south are continually tempered by the cold, nutrient-rich Hainan current which sweeps down from the north past Japan. The balance of cool and warm water varies according to season but the continued input of nutrients

and are served by ferries. Most of these leave Hong Kong Island from the Outlying Districts Services Pier, (Central). Two good routes to take are the ferry to Lantau, which normally stops off at the smaller island of Peng Chau, and the ferry to Cheung Chau. There is a good chance of seeing gulls, ospreys and white-bellied sea eagles as you approach the islands.

Mai Po Marshes

Mai Po Marshes offer some of the best birdwatching in Hong Kong. A patchwork of mangroves and brackish and tidal pools attracts vast numbers of water birds including waders, herons, egrets, terns and kingfishers. Not only are the numbers of birds impressive, but the variety is also outstanding. Over 250 species have been recorded, some of which are year-round residents while others are passage migrants or winter visitors.

Most of Mai Po is enclosed within the boundaries of an official nature reserve, managed by the World Wide Fund for Nature (Hong Kong). In order to visit the reserve, you must apply in advance to the World Wide Fund for Nature (Hong Kong), 1 Tramway Path, Central, Hong Kong (tel: 2526 4473). All visits are guided and take place at weekends and public holidays. Failing an organised visit, the ponds adjacent to the road from Mai Po village to the reserve entrance are still rich in birdlife. Visitors should always bear in mind the proximity of the border with the People's Republic of China and respect instructions

ensures that a healthy food chain is perpetuated.

Man is not the only mammal to exploit the harvest of the sea around Hong Kong, and, well away from the shore, large species of whale are occasionally seen. Closer to land, Chinese white dolphins and bottle-nosed dolphins sometimes bow-ride the boats, maintaining impressive bursts of speed.

Although most of the 235 outlying islands in the waters surrounding Hong Kong are uninhabited, some have small communities

PEACE AND QUIET

Great egrets are the largest marsh birds of the region

from the police, who are ever-alert for illegal immigrants. Throughout the year, the pools are thronged with Chinese pond-herons, little and great egrets, while ever-present are the black kites which scavenge any scraps from left-over meals. Common sandpipers wade in the shallow mud in search of invertebrates, and in the mangroves, white-breasted and common kingfishers perch on the look-out for fish below. Crested bulbuls, black-faced laughing-thrushes and white-eyes feed among the foliage of bushes. Magpie-robins, with their conspicuous black-and-white plumage, prefer more open areas.

From October to March, wintering birds such as bluethroat wryneck, and Richard's pipit feed around the dry, muddy margins to the pools. Waders too spend the winter here and in Deep Bay, but during migration time, their numbers and varieties increase dramatically, and it is not uncommon to see over 30 species in a single day. To reach Mai Po drive north from Kowloon to Tai Po. Turn left towards Yuen Long and then right onto Castle Peak Road. At Mai Po, a road to the left leads to a car park. There is an Exhibition Centre, a branch of the World Wide Fund for Nature and trails and hides.

Deep Bay

Deep Bay, in the far northwest of the New Territories, is one of Hong Kong's best birdwatching spots. Although the area may lack a little of the variety offered by the Mai Po Nature Reserve which it adjoins, it has the great advantage of being far more accessible. From the shoreline, on which some of the birds roost at high-tide, vast mudflats stretch away into the distance when the tide is out and provide a rich feeding ground for waders, ducks, terns and gulls.

In common with Mai Po, Deep Bay is especially good during spring and autumn migration time and many of the birds commute between the two sites. Up to 40 species of wader can be recorded in a single season, some of them being difficult to see anywhere else in the world, and fabled names like Nordmann's greenshank and spoon-billed sandpiper lure many migrant birdwatchers to stop off in Hong Kong on long-haul flights.

Deep Bay at low-tide presents a vast area of originally-rich mud on which the feeding birds are evenly spread, and consequently most are extremely distant. However, as the tide rises, they are pushed closer and closer to the shore and then provide much better views. To see the mudflats at their best, the stretch of coast between Lau Fau Shan and Tsim Bei Tsui is best and, beyond this point, visitors can continue on foot to within sight of Mai Po. During the winter, by scanning the bay at high tide or deep water channels at low tide, great-crested grebes, cormorants, red-breasted mergansers and even Dalmatian pelicans may be seen. Although regularly seen here, this last species is rare on a global scale and considered endangered. Pied kingfishers occasionally hover and plunge into the water after fish but are more regularly seen perched around coastal pools.

Teal, wigeon, shelduck and other dabbling duck prefer to feed on organisms in the exposed mud and are more easily seen at low tide. Black-headed gulls can be numerous and feed either by paddling the mud to disturb hidden animals or sometimes by coercing other birds into giving up their own meals. To reach Deep Bay, drive from Kowloon through Tuen Mun and then turn left to Lau Fau Shan. Continue along the road to the promontory at Tsim Bei Tsui.

Waders in Deep Bay

Although rich in all forms of water-loving birds, the mudflats of Deep Bay are especially renowned for the numbers and variety of waders that they support. Casual observers cannot fail to be impressed by the sight and sound of the huge winter flocks, and hardened enthusiasts, keen to identify the maximum number of species, and hopefully a few rarities, are seldom disappointed. Since most of the waders are either passage migrants, passing through in spring and autumn, or winter visitors from August until April, there is usually something of interest to be seen throughout the year.

Although to many people waders

tend to look rather similar, many of those that occur in Deep Bay are either well-marked or comparatively large and easily identified. Whimbrels and curlews with their long, down-curved beaks are not easily mistaken and black-tailed and bar-tailed godwits are recognised by their long, slightly up-curved beaks.

Smaller waders are also well represented and Kentish plovers and greater sand-plovers are numerous. Curlew sandpipers, easily picked out in flight by their white rumps, are also common, along with red-necked stints, but at least 10 potentially confusing species also occur regularly, so careful observations are necessary.

Many of these birds have rather specialised beaks which have evolved to suit their method of feeding. Perhaps most bizarre is the tiny spoon-billed sandpiper whose spatulate-tipped bill helps filter minute organisms from the mud. Terek sandpipers are also fascinating to watch as they chase along with their long, up-turned bills flicking from side to side. Their bright yellow legs are set so far back on their bodies that they give the impression that if they stopped moving they would fall over. Spotted redshanks are common passage migrants to Deep Bay, their loud 'kewick' call being distinctive. They are sometimes joined by redshank and greenshank, but pride of place must go to Nordmann's greenshank, a handful of which are seen each year. This bird can be distinguished from the more frequent greenshank by its

yellow legs, yellow base to the bill and webbed toes. Although identification requires patient observation, success means a real blue-riband for the birdwatcher.

Mangroves
Throughout the tropical regions of the world, river estuaries, mudflats and quiet backwaters support extraordinary swamp forests of mangrove. These evergreen trees are among the few plants capable of growing in the harsh conditions of choking silt and salty water and are so well-adapted to this environment that they are vital to the stabilisation of the mud and the creation of new land. Around the shores of Hong Kong, the mangroves are now much reduced due to the activities of man, but they can still be seen in places around Deep Bay and Mai Po.

Of the 30 or so species of mangrove which grow around the coasts of the South China Sea, each one is best suited to a different position on the shore according to the amount of salt or freshwater and the exposure to air at low tide which it can tolerate. The tangled network of roots, so characteristic of this habitat, served to anchor the plants in the shifting mud, and aerial roots facilitate gas exchange otherwise impossible in the sticky mud. The roots inadvertently trap more and more silt and are forced to extend higher and higher, and over a period of decades, this gradually consolidates the mud to form dry land.

The roots provide a haven for

many species of fish and crab. The curious mudskipper fish, capable of hopping around on bare mud, and fiddler crabs, the males with their brightly coloured pincers, dot the surface. The mangroves are also a safe nursery for young fish which, when full-grown, are open water species. Many of these are important commercial fish later in life and to destroy mangrove swamps not only wrecks a fascinating environment but also seriously

A few areas of mangrove swamp persist around the coast

affects the future prospects of many fisheries.

Mangroves also harbour a variety of birds; white-eyes forage among the foliage while, on the mud below, waders such as Kentish plover and red-necked stint feast on the invertebrate life found there. White-breasted kingfishers perch in the branches and dive down to capture fish and crabs, even when the water level is surprisingly low. By day, great and little egrets stalk patiently through the channels of water, while after dark they are replaced by night herons.

Tai Po Kau Nature Reserve

Lying above Tolo Harbour, Tai Po Kau Nature Reserve holds what is probably the best example of native woodland left in Hong Kong. Popular as a beauty spot with both residents and tourists, the rolling countryside is scenically attractive and the natural forests harbour a wealth of interesting plants and animals. In particular, the birdwatching within the reserve is excellent both for resident species and migrants, many of which are seldom recorded elsewhere in Hong Kong.

As with many other sites in Hong Kong, disturbance caused by people at weekends and on public holidays can make birdwatching difficult, especially in the vicinity of the car parks and picnic sites. However, a nature trail and several forest walks, colour-coded according to distance, allow those with a more serious interest to escape the noise and clamour.

Birdwatching in Tai Po Kau is good throughout the year but during migration, from March to May and August to October, the rewards may be unexpected and all the more exciting: after a short period of bad weather, the bushes can be alive with birds. Brown, blue-and-white and Asian paradise flycatchers may be among them, males of the last species being a particularly beautiful sight with their long, chestnut tails.

From October to March, the forests play host to a range of winter visitors. Red-throated, olive-backed and Richard's pipits feed in the open area or along the trails, sometimes in the company of pale and grey-backed thrushes. Mixed parties of warblers, flycatchers and other birds are also present.

Although many of Tai Po Kau's resident birds are shy and retiring, this is by no means true of all of them. Great barbets, with their green and chestnut plumage and yellow beaks, sometimes sit on bare branches, while black drongos draw attention to themselves with their hissing call and habit of perching in the open. Colourful Chinese blue (or red-billed) magpies are occasionally seen among the foliage, and resident scarlet minivets and treepies are also conspicuous, numbers of the latter two species being swollen in the winter by migrants. To reach Tai Po Kau nature reserve take the Tai Po Road from Ma Liu Shui. The entrance is clearly marked. There is a nature trail and several marked routes.

The Chinese blue magpie is perhaps one of Hong Kong's most attractive birds

Sai Kung Country Park

Set in the extreme east of the New Territories, the scenery of the Sai Kung Peninsula is among the finest in Hong Kong. Despite the creation of the High Island Reservoir within the boundaries of the Country Park, most of the park's landscape has probably changed little in centuries. Natural woodlands and scrub merge with grassland and plantations and, here and there, the remains of long-abandoned villages and temples add cultural interest.

Sai Kung can be reached from Hong Kong Island either on the coast road which runs to Tai Mong Tsai or by ferry. These run on a daily basis, but for more adventurous visitors, youth hostels and camp sites provide cheap bases from which to explore the park more thoroughly. For long- or medium- distance walks visitors can join the MacLehose Trail which for part of its length runs through the park. The trek eventually leads west away from Sai Kung and winds for 60 miles (100km) across eight country parks and through some wonderful scenery until it reaches Tuen Mun.

PEACE AND QUIET

Among the scrub and open woodland, the visitor will hear the grating call of the Chinese francolin. These partridge-like gamebirds often call from the open in spring but for the rest of the year are rather wary. This is not surprising, since they are frequently caught and can be found in most of Hong Kong's markets.

In spring and autumn, hundreds of tired migrant birds, including dollarbirds and flycatchers, pass through the park and mixed flocks of small passerines feed in the bushes. They join common resident birds such as greater coucal, great tit and white-eye, numbers of the latter species being boosted in winter by birds from the mainland. Chinese, red-vented and crested (red-whiskered) bulbuls are often seen, sometimes in quite large flocks. During the breeding season, however, the males are territorial and crested bulbuls in particular advertise their presence with a loud song.

On warm days, butterflies dance through the open woodland and lizards and snakes bask in the sun's rays. Fortunately for those with an aversion to snakes, most species are generally timid and retreat if disturbed. However, do not ever be tempted to try to handle one because at least eight of Hong Kong's species are highly venomous; these include the banded krait, the King cobra and the bamboo snake.

Parks and gardens are favoured habitats for the red-whiskered bulbul, a boldly marked bird

Lion Rock Country Park

Across the waters of Victoria Harbour, the Lion Rock Country Park is one of the first areas of countryside reached on leaving Hong Kong Island for the New Territories. The hill country which comprises the park's 1,300 acres (526 hectares) is dominated by Lion Rock itself, an outcrop of granite that, from some angles, resembles a crouched lion. Although decades of interference by man have reduced the park's woodland to a sorry state, a programme of intensive planting and conservation work is now underway to restore the natural cover.

Lion Rock has always been a popular destination for local residents and tourists alike. Outcrops such as Lion Rock, Mong Fu Shek and Beacon Hill provide wonderful views, but part of the park's attraction must lie in its comparative inaccessibility. Since no public roads run through the park, the only way in is on foot; fortunately there is no shortage of footpaths, some of which form part of the long-distance MacLehose Trail. Replanting of the woodlands has met with mixed success because fires and former land-use had already seriously impoverished the soil. However, Chinese red pine, strawberry tree and ivy tree are common and in the western half of the park, the planting has been deliberately varied to increase its value to wildlife. This is now a designated conservation area and a nature trail allows easy access.

In the wilder regions of the park, swallowtail butterflies flit along the paths while cicadas sing during spring and summer but are infuriatingly difficult to spot. Small parties of ring-necked (or rose-ringed) parakeets screech noisily through the scrub and occasionally breed where the trees are old enough and large enough to provide nesting holes. There is doubt as to whether the parakeets spread naturally to Hong Kong or were introduced to the colony, but whatever the case, they are now quite widespread.

The ubiquitous black kite is also common in the park, its whistling call and forked tail in flight making identification easy. They sometimes nest in the larger pines and their numbers demonstrate how this scavenging bird has profited from man's presence. Also benefiting from human company are the park's long-tailed macaques which, like those around Kowloon reservoir, have learned to accept food from tourists.

Kam Shan Country Park

To the north of Kowloon in the New Territories, the boundaries of Kam Shan Country Park enclose over 740 acres (300 hectares) of scrub and semi-natural woodland with much of the land comprising the catchment area for four reservoirs. This hilly park is dominated by the 980-ft (300m) Golden Hill and from here panoramic views can be had of Smuggler's Ridge, Lion Rock, Tai Mo Shan and distant towns and harbours.

Although only a single public road traverses the park, a whole network of signposted footpaths criss-crosses the countryside, allowing almost complete access to Kam Shan. Some of the paths even form part of the MacLehose Trail, the 60-mile (100km) trek which winds its way across most of the New Territories.

Whether you stroll gently around the shores of the reservoirs or through the open woodland of Chinese red pine and slash pine, you will come across a variety of colourful insects. April and May and October and November are the best months for butterflies, and brightly marked skippers and elegant and fast-flying swallowtails provide a dazzling spectacle. Close to the water, metallic dragonflies and damselflies chase smaller insects for food or each other to mate, during which process they fly around in random.

Woodland shrews are sometimes

PEACE AND QUIET

A skipper butterfly – one of Hong Kong's colourful insects

seen scurrying among the fallen leaves, but the most conspicuous mammals found in Kam Shan are the long-tailed (or pig-tailed) macaques. Although genuinely wild individuals are found elsewhere in Hong Kong, those along the wooded Tai Po Road are descendants of macaques reintroduced in 1920. Under natural conditions, their omnivorous diet would include everything from fruits and nuts to insects and small mammals. Like other monkeys, however, they are naturally inquisitive, especially with regard to food, and have learned to pester picnickers for scraps, which can cause considerable annoyance.

Completed in 1910, Kowloon Reservoir was the first to be built in the New Territories. Subsequently three smaller Reservoirs, Shek Lei Pui, Reception and Byewash, have been constructed. In addition to their scenic appeal, they are of interest to the birdwatcher, with migrant waders sometimes feeding around their margins and great-crested grebes and several species of duck being seen regularly on their waters.

Yim Tso Ha Egretry

Lying in the northeast of the New Territories, the Yim Tso Ha Egretry is a wonderful spectacle from April until August. Protected since 1969, hundreds of pairs of birds now make their twiggy nests among the bushes, whole trees becoming whitewashed with droppings by the end of the season. Although other egretries exist at Mong Tseng Wai and at Mai Po village, Yim Tso Ha is by far the best and most accessible.

The egretry is reached by taking the Tolo Highway north towards the border and turning right towards Sha Tau Kok, this road eventually running along the northern shore of Starling Inlet. At the southwestern end of the inlet, up to six species of heron and egret breed, including as many as 100 pairs of cattle egrets. During the breeding season these attractive birds are recognised by their buff throats and crowns and yellow legs and bills.

A few pairs of great egrets also breed in among the larger numbers of night herons and elegantly-plumed little egrets. The more observant visitors may spot one of the few pairs of the endangered Swinhoe's egret, which breed at Yim Tso Ha. Distinguished by its yellow toes and bill and blue-grey facial skin, this is one of the world's rarest birds.

FOOD AND DRINK

A rich and varied eating adventure can be undertaken in the cornucopia of Hong Kong's restaurants. The cuisines of China, southeast Asia, India, Pakistan, Japan, Korea and Europe are all represented, and standards are high.

Chinese

Whatever the regional cuisine, it aims to maintain a delicate balance between the positive (*yang*) and negative (*ying*) forces of the universe, as advocated by the ancient Taoists. This is created, in Chinese food, by the harmonious ordering of dishes, which should produce the

Restaurants, such as this one in Kowloon, offer a wide selection of meats to tempt you

correct healthy balance of cold and hot, bland and spicy, sour and sweet. The dietary principles of Chinese cuisine were established many centuries ago, and though they may appear mere superstition to many young Chinese, they are nevertheless still adhered to. The foods which are said to have aphrodisiac qualities – snake bladder, ginseng and chicken, steamed carp – are very expensive. It is said that eggplant can cause female infertility and pig's brain can cause male impotence. Snake soup with shredded chrysanthemum petals is considered a great winter restorative. Other expensive dishes are eaten for their texture – bird's nests and *bêche-de-mer* – which does not normally appeal to the foreign palate.

FOOD AND DRINK

A Chinese dinner is best enjoyed with as many people as possible; and the principle of one course per person and one extra will ensure the right amount of dishes. The waiter can be asked for his personal recommendation. Prices for seasonal specialities and fresh seafood should be ascertained, for these items can be very expensive. Restaurants are very helpful in making suggestions for a balanced textured and tasty meal.

If you should be hosting a dinner with Chinese guests, the correct seating etiquette puts the guest of honour facing the door, with the host seated opposite. A local Hong Kong tradition, of never turning a fish over when eating it, is a superstition of the fishing community, who fear that a fishing boat will capsize at sea. Fruit and hot towels will indicate the end of the meal and Chinese guests do not expect to linger at the table beyond this stage.

The ordinary man-in-the-street will take his meals at the streetside noodle stalls and snack shops serving all sorts of seafood, rice dishes and noodle soups; simply point out what you fancy. A more refined, typically Cantonese style of eating is 'taking tea' (*yum cha*) with *dim sum*. It is different from other kinds of Chinese eating in that tea is drunk throughout the whole meal. Restaurants serving these small snacks are warm and friendly, and are packed out from early morning till lunchtime. The delicacies are wheeled around the restaurant in trolleys. Simply indicate which delicacy you would like from the passing

One of Aberdeen's floating eateries: the Jumbo Floating Restaurant

trolley lady, who will place the dish or steamed basket before you and mark the card on your table appropriately.

Just a few of the popular *dim sum* dishes are listed below.

Cha Siu Bau: steamed barbecued pork bun

Siu Mei: steamed meat dumplings

Har Gua: steamed shrimp dumplings

Chun Kuen: spring rolls
Pai Kwat: steamed spareribs with red pepper sauce
Ho Yip Fan: steamed fried rice wrapped in lotus leaf
Jar Wan Tun: deep fried dumplings with sweet and sour sauce
Nor Mai Chee: coconut snowball
Hung Dow Sa: sweet red bean soup
Ngor Mai Chee: sweet rice dumplings with shredded coconut
Woo Kok: deep-fried taro rolls stuffed with vegetables
Daan Tart: egg-custard tart.

Cantonese
The foremost Chinese cuisine in Hong Kong is Cantonese style, originating in the nearby province of Guangdong. Dishes emphasise fresh ingredients and natural flavour and colour. Steaming and stir frying are favoured and a minimum of oil is used. They also have a tasty barbecued meat tradition. The province's long South China Sea

FOOD AND DRINK

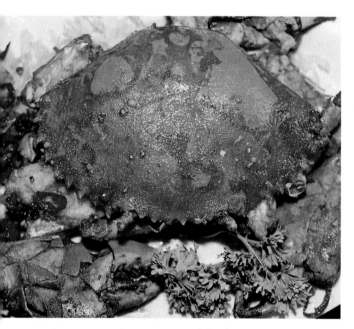

Baked mud-crab, one of Hong Kong's seafood-based Chinese dishes

coastline is rich in seafood and many restaurants keep tanks of live fish, crabs and shellfish. A popular sub-category of Cantonese food is *Chiu Chow* cuisine, originating in the Swatow (Shantou) region of northeastern Guangdong province. The piquant flavourings of seafood, goose and duck are delicious. *Chiu Chow* meals begin and end with thimble-size cups of strong Iron Goddess tea. Local seafood specialities can also be enjoyed on the floating restaurants near Aberdeen, and at the villages of Lei Yue Mun and Lau Fau Shan in the New Territories.

Below is a selection of Cantonese restaurants:-

Chiuchow Garden, Basement, Jardine House, Connaught Road Central (tel: 2525 8246). An extensive menu of *Chiu Chow* specialities which include fried satay beef, steamed pomfret fish with soya bean sauce, and roast goose with vinegar and garlic. Shark's-fin dishes are always a showcase for *Chiu Chow* chefs.

Jade Garden, 1st Floor, Swire House, 11 Chater Road, Central (tel: 2526 3031); 4th Floor, Star House, 3 Salisbury Road, Tsim Sha Tsui, Kowloon (tel: 2730 6888); and 1 Hysan Avenue, Causeway Bay (tel: 2577 9332). Service is matter of fact and speedy with menus of standard Cantonese dishes and seasonal delicacies, particularly seafood. These include barbecued pork, deep-fried stuffed crab claws, fillet of fish in lemon sauce, sautéed spiced prawns and the ever popular beggar's chicken baked in mud (this must be pre-ordered).

Loong Yuen, Basement, Holiday Inn Golden Mile Hotel, 46–52 Nathan Road, Tsim Sha Tsui (tel: 2369 3111). This is a good place to enjoy first-class Cantonese food, plus an interesting selection of other regional specialities, with a menu in English and staff will happily describe and recommend dishes you may not be familiar with.

Luk Yu Tea House, 26 Stanley Street, Central (tel: 2523 5464). Famed for its old teahouse atmosphere since 1925, it serves excellent *dim sum*. There are no English menus but the waiters are helpful and recommend seasonal specials.

Tai Woo, 15–19 Wellington Street, Central (tel: 2524 5618); 27 Percival Street, Causeway Bay (tel: 2893 9882); and 14–16 Hillwood Road, Tsim Sha Tsui, Kowloon (tel: 2369 9773). Excellent Cantonese dishes and *dim sum* make this group of restaurants popular for family banquets. Choice of set meals or seasonal dishes. Try braised cuttlefish, braised beef, crispy beancurd rolls and vegetarian hotpot.

Tao Yuan, 3rd Floor, Great Eagle Centre, 23 Harbour Road, Wan Chai (tel: 2827 8080). Graciously decorated and serving subtle, home-style Cantonese dishes with many seasonal specialities, plus an exciting *dim sum* menu.

Yung Kee Restaurant, 32–40 Wellington Street, Central (tel: 2522 1624). A restaurant of long-standing high repute whose seafood dishes – pomfret with chilli and black bean sauce, scallops, and grilled prawns – are recommended. Roast goose is the house speciality, while special winter dishes include snake soup served with preserved duck.

Peking

This is a substantial cuisine, suited to the colder climes of China's northern capital, and influenced by the tastes of the court. Peking duck is the most famous delicacy and the golden roasted bird is shown to the table for approval before slicing. It is eaten wrapped up in thin pancakes with a sprig of spring onion and cucumber. Mongolian hot pot, served with a sauce mixed from seven ingredients and sesame rolls, is a winter favourite. Beggar's chicken is a speciality of many Peking restaurants in Hong Kong. Dumplings, noodles and steamed breads are preferred staples. If you are planning to eat Peking duck or beggar's chicken it is best to advise the restaurant when you book your table in order to avoid disappointment.

American Restaurant, 20 Lockhart Road, Wan Chai (tel: 2527 1000). An unlikely name for a restaurant with good and reliable Peking dishes which include Peking duck, onion bread, chilli prawns, shredded pork with green pepper, diced chicken with soya bean sauce, and Tsientsin cabbage in chicken oil.

FOOD AND DRINK

Prices are most reasonable but book in advance.

Hong Kong Chung Chuk Lau, 30 Leighton Road, Causeway Bay (tel: 2577 4914). This restaurant serves authentic Mongolian hot pot during the winter. The Peking style is to order one kind of meat only, either mutton or beef, but the Cantonese adaptation includes meat, fish and chicken. The thin slivers of meat are literally rinsed in broth in the charcoal heated hot pot, to which is added vegetables, beancurd and noodles. After cooking the meat is dipped into a seven-flavour sauce and eaten with sesame rolls. Typical Peking dishes are also served.

Peking Garden, 1st and 2nd Basement, Alexandra House, 16 Ice House Street, Central (tel: 2526 6456); 1st Floor, Excelsior Hotel Shopping Arcade, 281 Gloucester Road, Causeway Bay (tel: 2577 7231); and 3rd Floor, Star House, 3 Salisbury Road, Tsim Sha Tsui, Kowloon (tel: 2735 8211). These restaurants are reliable and smart. Guests always enjoy the chef's nightly demonstrations in the skill of noodle making.

Their menus include cold meat, famous Peking duck, duck soup, smoked chicken, fried minced pork with Chinese pickles, and grilled mutton with spring onion.

Spring Deer, 1st Floor, 42 Mody Road, Tsim Sha Tsui, Kowloon (tel: 2723 3673). Locals prefer this restaurant, considering its Peking duck the best available. Also try the chicken with chilli and sweet peppers, and sour-hot chilli prawns.

Shanghai

Shanghainese food tends to be oily, rich and with a tendency towards sweetness. Steamed dumplings are traditional fare, but seasonal specialities, such as eels with garlic and freshwater 'hairy' crabs are delicious autumn treats. These small crabs are flown down live in huge quantities from Shanghai – the females, with their fat roe, are more expensive than the males. Hot ginger-flavoured tea is served at the end of a crab feast.

Great Shanghai, 1st Floor, 26 Prat Avenue, Tsim Sha Tsui, Kowloon (tel: 2366 8158). A friendly and comfortable restaurant, much esteemed by gourmets of Shanghainese cuisine with a choice of over 400 dishes. Its drunken chicken (cold chicken pieces flavoured with coriander and yellow rice wine) is a speciality of the house, as are its eel dishes, ideally accompanied by heated Shanghainese wine.

Shanghai Garden, 115–24 and 126 Hutchison House, 10 Harcourt Road, Central (tel: 2524 8181). Yangtse River dishes and seafood – sautéed scallops with vegetables, stewed shrimps with tomato sauce and crispy rice, steamed fish – as well as steamed and fried dumplings, served in elegant surroundings.

Sichuan (Szechuan)

The hot, spicy cuisine of this western province of China is one of the four main styles of Chinese cooking and is famous world-wide, as its piquancy appeals to many palates. Peppers, coriander, ginger and garlic are basic ingredients for Sichuan dishes.

Kam Chuen Lau, 4 Observatory Road, Tsim Sha Tsui, Kowloon (tel: 2367 5629). The Sichuan (or Szechuan) style camphor wood and tea leaf smoked duck is this restaurant's speciality, along with other dishes such as fried shrimps with salt, deep fried beef with chilli and celery, and Sichuan bacon and leeks.

Red Pepper, 7 Lan Fong Road, Causeway Bay (tel: 2576 8046). Popular family-run restaurant. Try the sizzling prawns or the distinctive 'strange taste' spiced, shredded chicken.

Sichuan Garden, 3rd Floor, Gloucester Tower, The Landmark, 11 Pedder Street, Central (tel: 2521 4433). Very good but expensive. Their menu offers crispy fried shredded beef with chilli, Yunnan ham and lotus-seeds in honey sauce, fried spiced spare ribs, hot *mapo* beancurd and delicious camphor wood and tea smoked duck.

Sze Chuen Lau, 466 Lockhart Road, Causeway Bay (tel: 2891 9027). In this well-established restaurant, the service is brisk and efficient and prices reasonable. Hot red lychee tea is served to each guest as well as hot cabbage and sweet cucumber pickles as starters. Try

Cuttlefish and octopuses are among the delicacies on display in a restaurant larder

FOOD AND DRINK

the silver thread steamed bread rolls or fried onion bread instead of rice – also frog's leg dishes (seasonal), camphor-flavoured tea-smoked duck, braised beef in chilli and try the mashed red bean pancake for dessert.

Vegetarian

The Buddhist and Taoist qualities of restraint and purity lie at the heart of Chinese vegetarian cooking. Beancurd is widely used and often made to look like meat. Chinese vegetarian meals are light and filling and aesthetically pleasing. Buddhist monks are frequently to be seen eating in these restaurants. See also the Indian restaurants on page 82 for vegetarian possibilities.
Bodhi Vegetarian Restaurant, 81, Nathan Road, Tsim Sha Tsui (tel: 2366 8283), serves a wide variety of Cantonese-style vegetarian dishes. The menu is pleasantly reassuring for non-vegetarians, featuring familiar 'meat' dishes.
Vegi Food Kitchen, Highland Mansion, 13–15 Cleveland Street, Causeway Bay (tel: 2890 6660). A small restaurant, always well patronised, where the service is both pleasant and helpful. Delicious choices include stuffed black mushrooms, beancurd dishes and beancurd skin rolls.
Kung Tak Lam Vegetarian Cuisine, 31 Yee Wo Street, Causeway Bay (tel: 2890 3127). The unique flavours of Shanghainese vegetarian food can be enjoyed in this reasonably priced restaurant, opposite Victoria Park. Try the rich taste of the 'eight treasures' platter and the spicy hot-and-sour soup.

Meats laid out at market, ready for the Chinese New Year

Asian

Hong Kong could be described as a cross-roads of Asian cuisine for there are restaurants serving authentic national dishes from all parts of the region. Even Japanese food, usually notoriously expensive, is affordable here. Korean barbecued beef, sharp and spicy Thai and Vietnamese soups and salads, and curries from Indonesia, Burma, India and Sri

Lanka, make a pleasant change from Chinese food.

Spices, 109 Repulse Bay Road (tel: 2812 2711) has menus offering a cross-section of southeast Asian cuisine Buffet spreads provide a bargain-priced way to sample the culinary delights of each region.

Indonesian

Java Rijsttafel, 38 Hankow Road, Tsim Sha Tsui, Kowloon (tel: 2367 1230). A traditional Indonesian rice table buffet is served each luncheon, and this includes fish sambal, spiced beef, vegetables with coconut milk and chicken curry.

Shinta Indonesian Food Wisma Club, 1st Floor, 36–44 Kar Yau Building, Queen's Road East, Wan Chai (tel: 2527 4974). There is not much attempt at atmosphere here, but the satays, brought with little charcoal burners to your table, are very tasty, as is their *gado-gado* salad, *nasi goreng* rice, spiced Rendang beef and chilli fried prawns. Prices are most reasonable.

FOOD AND DRINK

Indian

Ashoka, 57 Wyndham Street, Central (tel: 2525 5719). The selection of food from Kashmir and the Punjab at the Ashoka has made it a long-time favourite among lovers of Indian food. Apart from dishes such as tandoori chicken, beef and mutton curries and vegetable kofta and masala, the restaurant serves an assortment of meat or vegetarian dishes on a tray, which is perfect for a lone diner or for those who want to try everything.

Gaylord, First Floor, Ashley Centre, 23–25 Ashley Road, Tsim Sha Tsui (tel: 2376 1001). Indian food has been served here for over 20 years and its reputation remains undiminished. Curries and tandoori dishes are the specialities, with excellent starters like *chowpatty chaat*. At lunch time a buffet is served.

Woodlands, Ground Floor, Mirror Tower, 61 Mody Road, Tsim Sha Tsui (tel: 2369 3718). This is the only Indian vegetarian restaurant in Hong Kong, open since 1981 and still delighting customers with tasty and inexpensive meals. The *dosa* (rice flour pancakes) and *thali* set meals provide a good introduction to this healthy cuisine. No alcohol is served.

Japanese

Kanetanaka, 22nd Floor, East Point Centre, 545–563 Hennessy Road, Causeway Bay (tel: 2833 6018). Long established restaurant, popular with Japanese locals and visitors alike, with a wide choice of set meals or *à la carte*.

Yagiu Restaurant, 13–17 Stanley Street, Central (tel: 2523 9522). An unpretentious restaurant where the prices are most reasonable – for Japanese food, that is.

One may sit at the *sushi* bar around *tappanyaki* tables, or take a small cubicle. The menu offers a range of set dinners as well as *à la carte* ordering and, of course, hot Japanese rice wine (*saki*).

Korean

Arirang Korean Restaurant, 76 Morrison Hill Road, Happy Valley (tel: 2572 3027). The traditional Korean barbecue, cooked at your table, always makes for a friendly and pleasant evening's dining, and this restaurant offers some 20 different types of marinated meat and seafood to choose from. An unfussy and brightly decorated restaurant.

Koreana, Vienna Mansion, 55 Paterson Street, Causeway Bay (tel: 2577 5145). This has a pleasant, smoky atmosphere, and the hot pepper cabbage (*kimchee*), served with each meal, soon raises one's body temperature! Cook your own marinated chicken, beef, pork or shrimp barbecue at the table.

Thai

Golden Elephant Thai Restaurant, Harbour City, 17 Canton Road, Tsim Sha Tsui, Kowloon (tel: 2735 0733). All the chefs are trained in Thailand and the atmosphere is authentic. Specialities include sliced boneless goose, spicy and sour abalone salad, oyster omelette and charcoal grilled chicken.

Supatra's Thai Gourmet, Lan Kwai Fong, 50 D'Aguilar Street,

Chinese biscuits. Sweet and savoury snacks are set out on street stalls

Central (tel: 2522 5073). A popular Thai restaurant with character. The appetising menu includes fish cakes, spicy and sour prawn soup, green curry with roasted duck, curried pork in coconut, spicy squid salad and Thai fried rice.

Pan Asian

Viceroy, Second Floor, Sun Hung Kai Centre, 30 Harbour Road, Wan Chai (tel: 2827 7777). The menu is an exotic mix of Indian, Thai and Indonesian dishes. The interior is nothing special so ask for an outdoor table that overlooks Victoria harbour.

Stanley's Oriental, 90B Stanley Main Street, Stanley (tel: 2813 9988). A Pan-Earth menu of Japanese, Thai, Indian, Creole and Cajun dishes served facing the beach.

Mabuhay, 11 Minden Avenue, Tsim Sha Tsui, (tel: 2367 3762). This is a very friendly and inexpensive restaurant that serves authentic Filipino and Spanish food.

Golden Gate, First Floor, Multifield Plaza, 3–7 Prat Avenue, Tsim, Sha Tsui (tel: 2723 1389).

FOOD AND DRINK

Indian, Thai, Malay and Indonesian dishes at reasonable prices. The Indian and *satay* food is delicious.

Western

La Brasserie, Basement, Omni Marco Polo Hotel, Harbour City, Canton Road, Tsim Sha Tsui (tel: 2737 7925). A delightful Parisian atmosphere that offers relief and release from the hectic crowds of shoppers outside. The menu can be found on a mirror near the entrance and changes regularly. Meat and seafood dishes are excellent.

Grissini, Grand Hyatt, 1 Harbour Road, Wan Chai (tel: 2588 1234). The superb North Italian food served here is complemented by equally fine views of the harbour.

Bentley's Seafood Restaurant, B4, Basement, Prince's Building, 10 Chater Road, Central (tel: 2868 0881). A member of the Bentley's Seafood Restaurant chain of London, it recreates a conservative and quiet British atmosphere, which is reflected in the menu – first class but simple seafood dishes.

Café de Paris, 30–32 California Tower, D'Aguilar Street, Central (tel: 2524 7521). Its chic décor, high standard of cuisine and good selection of wines make this excellent value.

Chesa, Peninsula Hotel, Salisbury Road, Tsim Sha Tsui, Kowloon (tel: 2366 6251), together with **Gaddi's** in the same hotel, are two leading restaurants; the former serves superb Swiss food and the latter first class French dishes. Both restaurants have lush and elegant surroundings, and both are, of course,

expensive. Gaddi's special executive lunch menu is, however, good value.

Jimmy's Kitchen, Basement, South China Building, 1 Wyndham

Taking refreshments in lofty company in front of the Repulse Bay Temple

Street, Central (tel: 2526 5293).
Jimmy's Kitchen started as a
seaman's café in Shanghai in
the 1940s and moved to Hong
Kong with its staff. The
atmosphere in the restaurant is
cosy and reassuring, and the
menu contains a special blend
of east and west, reflecting its

China-coast tradition. Prices are
reasonable.

La Taverna, Ground Floor,
Astoria Building, 36–38 Ashley
Road, Tsim Sha Tsui, Kowloon
(tel: 2376 1945) and 1st Floor,
Shun Ho Tower, 24–30 Ice House
Street, Central (tel: 2522 8904).
The atmosphere is typically
Mediterranean and the Italian
dishes, though erratic in quality,
are fresh and appetising.
Specialities are pizzas, seafood
and desserts.

Pierrot, Mandarin Oriental Hotel,
5 Connaught Road, Central (tel:
2522 0111). Very elegant and
expensive autumn coloured
restaurant. Excellent and delicate
service with dishes and wine to
match.

Stanley's French Restaurant,
86 Stanley Main Street, Stanley
(tel: 2813 8873). Delightfully
situated, overlooking Stanley
Bay, this restaurant's Provençal-
style French menu, though not
extensive, is first class.

Drink

Drinking wine while composing
poetry was the favoured pastime
of the Chinese literati for
centuries. Today drinking is still
an important part of the
enjoyment of a Chinese banquet.
The standard Cantonese toast is
Yum sing! (meaning 'Cheers!').
Traditionally golden yellow rice
wine from Shaoxing is preferred.
This sherry-like wine is aged in
earthenware jars for up to seven
years and is served warm from
wine jugs and poured into small
wine cups.
The fiery white *sorghum* liquor
called *mao tai* is popular too, but
in recent years, this special hard
liquor from Kweichow province,

FOOD AND DRINK

Tea is always taken with Chinese meals. This herbal tea shop is in Hong Kong Island's Western District

and a favourite of the late Chairman Mao Tsetung, has become scarce and too expensive. So local people drink substitutes such as *fen jiu (fen chiew)* and *wu liang ye*. Unlike Shaoxing wine, these distilled liquors do not usually appeal to the western palate. Other Chinese wines, often sweet and unusual in flavour, include Green Bamboo Leaf Wine, Rose Nectar and Tiger Bone Papaya wine. However, the most favoured drink with Chinese meals among the affluent Hong Kong people these days is French Cognac, and the territory is among the highest consumers of VSOP brandy in the world. European restaurants serve imported French, German, Italian and Australian wines. Cocktail bars and nightclubs serve an assortment of both traditional and creative cocktails. The local beer, San Miguel, is a lager-like brew, and is light and popular, but many imported beers are available.

SHOPPING

Seven million tourists a year cannot be wrong – Hong Kong is an amazing place to shop. The streets and alleys are jammed with air-conditioned shops and market stalls stocking an overwhelming array of goods, both imported and locally made. Many goods are cheaper here than in their place of origin, due to duty free imports, and this applies particularly to goods from mainland China.
For those who love the challenge of bargaining over prices, Hong Kong is a delight which may reward your time and determination with more than satisfactory value-for-money purchases. But those who are disinclined to haggle with aggressive sales staff may find the process irritating and distasteful, and simply pay roughly what is asked in the interest of time-saving.
Once you are in Hong Kong it is doubly important to shop around on prices, for the same object can vary widely in price. The lowest price may not necessarily mean the best quality – slightly defective goods may be foisted on you to make up for any big discount.
Of the thousands of shops only some 970 are members of the Hong Kong Tourist Association and display their 'red junk' logo. These stores are considered to be highly reputable, but this does not mean that Hong Kong business people are not mostly honest and conscientious. Your purchases may be discussed over proffered cigarettes or cups of Chinese tea which lends amiability to the negotiations! Always check carefully that the goods are

packed before your eyes and that you have received exactly the component parts and accessories you wanted. *Never* pay a deposit on goods which have to be fetched from the warehouse; and check your receipt carefully – once you have accepted it you have very little recourse. Ask for world-wide guarantees where possible.
The Hong Kong Tourist Association's *Shopping* guide is a comprehensive introduction to Hong Kong's shopping world. There are three principal shopping areas: downtown Kowloon in Tsim Sha Tsui and Tsim Sha Tsui East, Hong Kong Island's Central District and the Causeway Bay area. Having said this, the Yau Ma Tei and Mong Kok districts (accessible by MTR) offer good bargains too. Obviously, the more central the shop, the more its massive rental overheads affect prices. Trading hours are usually from 10.00–18.00 daily (though some shops close on Sunday), but many shops will stay open till 19.30 or even 21.30 in the evening.

Cameras and Optical Equipment
The latest models and accessories are on sale in the many, many shops dealing in this trade. The staff are very knowledgeable and anxious to assist. Discounts of 5-15 per cent or so can be arranged. To avoid later disappointment, note that the serial number of the equipment checks out with the guarantee. Binoculars are particularly good buys. James Morgan has written a booklet

aptly named: *How to Avoid Getting Ripped-Off in Hong Kong Buying Cameras and Photo Accessories,* which is available at many bookstores.

Free and accurate eye tests are carried out in the optician stores and prescription glasses and contact lenses can be made in a very short time. The cost is more than reasonable.

Electronic Equipment

There are sound systems galore to tempt you, as well as all the latest electronic games and gadgetry of our age. Always check the voltage of equipment and the compatibility of VHS systems.

Computers represent good value and the second floor of **Star House**, 3 Salisbury Road, Tsim Sha Tsui (near the Star ferry) has a wide choice of high quality software and hardware.

Jewellery

Second in number only to camera shops are jewellery stores. Favourite targets of smash-and-grab robbers, they nonetheless do a flourishing business. Local jewellery excels in craftsmanship and design and pieces can be custom made. Prices are very competitive. Gold and jade are traditionally popular with Chinese buyers. Translucent green or 'mutton fat' white are particularly favoured colours but jade also comes in many other beautiful colours. There are two types of jade: jadeite – used in jewellery – and nephrite for carvings. Most of the high quality jade comes from Burma. Kowloon's **Jade Market** in Yau Ma Tei district is an intriguing

Hong Kong has shops crammed with curios and reproduced 'antiques'

place to buy cheap pieces of jade jewellery.

The diamond trade in Hong Kong is one of the world's largest, so prices are low. For detailed information on cut, colour and carat weight contact the **Diamonds Importers Association Ltd**, Room 1102, Parker House, 72 Queen's Road, Central (tel: 2523 5497). A wide selection of pearls – cultured, fresh-water and baroque – ranges in price according to their quality and size. Your

choice of colouring – milk white, ivory, pale pink or grey – depends upon your preference. Pearls can be strung for you within hours. Semi-precious stones too are in abundance. The various branches of **Chinese Arts and Crafts** sell attractive but conservative jewellery.

Clothing and Fabrics
The rag trade is still a mainstay of the Hong Kong economic miracle and that entire spectrum of ready-to-wear apparel, from the cheapest T-shirt to the most expensive high fashion European labels,

are available, the latter being very popular with Japanese tourists. In recent years Hong Kong's own designers have earned international acclaim. Couturier boutiques are to be found, cheek by jowl, in the smart shopping complexes of the Landmark, Prince's Building and Swire House in Central. In Kowloon the shopping arcades of the Peninsula and Regent hotels are centres for international elegance. Two local designers have carved a world reputation: **Diane Freis** for lovely soft, uncrushable and colourful dresses and separates; and **Jenny Lewis**, who has an eye for

SHOPPING

old Chinese fabrics and embroideries, and creates beautiful gowns and jackets with strong oriental motifs.

Clothing with designer labels – jeans, sportswear and men's shirts – can be bought very cheaply in the street bazaars, particularly at Stanley Market, on the south side of Hong Kong Island.

Factory outlets sell their export overruns of knitwear, silk garments, leatherwear and accessories, from their factory premises in the industrial districts of Kwun Tong, Lai Chi Kok or San Po Kong (accessible by MTR). Other factories have premises in downtown Kowloon and in Central, and goods sell at wholesale prices. *The Complete Guide to Factory Bargains* by Diana Göetz, is updated every year and is on sale at bookshops. The HKTA also prints a useful listing.

Custom-tailored garments, for men and women, can be fitted and completed within a few days, though the workmanship may be better if the tailor can take a bit longer over them. Two or three fittings are advised. Garments can also be given to the tailor to copy. Usually a 50 per cent non-refundable deposit will be asked once your measurements have been noted.

Tailoring shops have selections of fabrics for you to choose from. For a vast choice of British wools, cashmere, silks, cottons and synthetics, the second floor of the Western Market in Sheung Wan, is the place. Pure silks from China are available by the metre at the **Chinese Arts and Crafts** department stores, as well as cotton and silk garments, embroideries and cashmere sweaters.

Shoes

Visitors can have shoes custom-made at reasonable prices. Fittings are desirable to ensure comfort and satisfaction. Ready-made local fashion shoes can be tried on at the numerous shoe-shops which trade side by side on a section of Wong Nai Chung Road, Happy Valley. Matching handbags make nice accessories.

Watches

Hong Kong's own watch industry produces attractive and accurate timepieces while the colony is a major importer of famous Swiss and Japanese brands. If choosing an expensive watch make sure that the serial number of the watch corresponds with its international guarantee, and try to make sure that the band is the original one (it may affect the guarantee).

Furniture

Hand carved teak, rosewood and blackwood furniture is made with a high degree of skill and taste and Chinese craftsmen can be seen at work in furniture shops on Queen's Road East and Hollywood Road on Hong Kong Island. Handsome dining suites, occasional tables or camphor wood chests can be custom-made and safe shipment arranged.

In recent years the simple lines of Ming Dynasty northern Chinese furniture have become more popular than the heavily carved pieces typical of southern China. Cane and rattan furniture is also made.

Carpets

Fine Chinese wool or silk carpets are often cheaper to buy here than in China. Hong Kong's **Tai Ping Carpets** make quality carpets in modern or traditional designs and are happy to make to personal requirements; their showroom is at Hutchison House, 10 Harcourt Road, Central (tel: 2522 7138). Other carpet shops specialise in antique tribal rugs

The temptation of the market stalls, with their fresh produce, can sometimes prove too much...

from Persia and Afghanistan, or modern carpets from Pakistan and India.

Antiques

Hollywood Road and Wyndham Street in Central is the home of Asian antiques and art works. Galleries elegantly display antique paintings, furniture, imperial costumes, ivory, pottery and porcelain. Unfortunately, there are not many bargains these days, even in the famous old 'Cat Street' (Upper Lascar Road) antique market.

SHOPPING

Shops spill out onto the street in Hollywood Road and Bird Street in Central

Antiques and modern reproductions frequently stand side by side.

Treasures continue to be smuggled from the mainland and it is sometimes possible to find painted pottery pots which are over 2,000 years old.

On Kowloon side, **Charlotte Horstmann & Gerald Godfrey** in the Ocean Terminal has a reputation for genuine, quality antiques.

Handicrafts

Delicate paper cuts, peasant woodcuts, weavings, puppets, embroideries, lacquer, stone carvings, tableware and basketry are just some of the traditional handicrafts from China to be found at the **Chinese Arts and Crafts** department stores, and at **Mountain Folk Craft** shops on both sides of the harbour.

The **Banyan Tree** and **Amazing Grace Elephant Company** deal in furnishings and hand crafted decorative objects which come from various countries in Asia.

ACCOMMODATION

Most of the territory's hotels are first class, both in décor, service and facilities. The lobbies are elegantly and lavishly decorated. Many are well appointed, offering stunning views of Hong Kong harbour. Hotels maintain a 75 per cent occupancy rate all year round. Rooms are air-conditioned with bathroom, TV, mini-bar and refrigerator.

Hotel restaurants serve Chinese and Western cuisine of a high standard. Some of the colony's very best restaurants are located in the top hotels. Conference rooms, business centres, swimming pools, private dining halls and discos are among the many facilities most Hong Kong hotels offer.

The more moderately priced hotels also tend to have good service and pleasant, small rooms, but the likelihood is that they will have no view.

Room rates quoted below are subject to a 15 per cent add-on (10 per cent service; 5 per cent tax) and these prices are obviously subject to change.

Hong Kong Island

Excelsior Hotel, 281 Gloucester Road, Causeway Bay (tel: 2894 8888). A very comfortable hotel, with high standards of service, situated in a busy shopping and restaurant area. Its sports facilities include tennis courts and a health club. It has two restaurants and three bars, of which the Dickens Bar is a popular spot for residents, as is the 'Talk of the Town' nightclub. It has 910 rooms which range from HK$1,400–HK$2,100 a double.

Hotel Furama Kempinski, 1 Connaught Road, Central (tel: 2525 5111). One of Central's leading hotels, close to the Star Ferry. Its revolving restaurant La Ronda on the top floor is a special attraction and the buffet lunch or dinner is highly recommended. There are four restaurants and two bars. Most of its 517 rooms have a view and rates are HK$1,700– HK$2,350 a double.

Harbour Hotel, 116–122 Gloucester Road, Wan Chai (tel: 2574 8211). This moderately priced hotel on the waterfront in the nightclub area of Wan Chai has a relaxed atmosphere. Its Chinese restaurant serves good, plain dishes. The hotel's other facilities include a bar and nightclub. The hotel's 200 rooms are priced at HK$500–HK$950 a double.

Harbour View International House, 4 Harbour Road, Wan Chai (tel: 2802 0111). Ideally situated on the waterfront, there is a free shuttle bus to Causeway Bay and the Star Ferry. The hotel has one restaurant and there are 320 rooms ranging from HK$850–HK$1,250.

J W Marriott Hotel, Pacific Place, 88 Queensway, Central (tel: 2810 8366). The views of the harbour and mountains from the rooms, with two of their walls being sheer glass, are unsurpassed. Facilities include a swimming pool and fitness centre. The hotel is also justly famous for its Californian restaurant. Rooms are HK$1,820–HK$2,450.

Mandarin Oriental Hotel, 5 Connaught Road, Central (tel: 2522 0111). Part of a hotel group which operates some of the best

ACCOMMODATION

hotels in Asia, the Mandarin is considered the leading one on the island. Apart from a health club, swimming pool and business centre, its Clipper Lounge is popular for afternoon tea, and the clientele of the Captain's Bar is made up of the community's leading businessmen. Restaurants include an excellent French restaurant, and a grill room. Its 542 rooms are priced at HK$2,000–HK$2,950 a double.

New Harbour Hotel, 41–49 Hennessy Road, Wan Chai (tel: 2861 1166). The 173 rooms are small and functional, as is the restaurant, bar and coffee shop. Situated in the centre of Wan Chai, the hotel's room rates cover a price range of HK$980–HK$1,300 a double.

The Park Lane, 310 Gloucester Road, Causeway Bay (tel: 2890 3355). A spacious hotel close to Vogue Alley and Causeway Bay shopping, its various facilities include several restaurants, coffee shop, disco, and sauna. It has 815 rooms.
Prices: HK$1,800–HK$3,100 a double.

Ritz-Carlton, 3 Connaught Road, Central (tel: 2877 6666). A slender building, resembling the Empire State Building but a lot smaller, that aims for quality rather than quantity. Period furniture in the rooms and a choice of views: Chater Gardens, Victoria Peak, or the harbour. There are four restaurants, including the superb Tuscano serving northern Italian cuisine. Rates for the 216 rooms are priced HK$2,200–HK$4,950, depending on the type of view from the room.

Kowloon

Bangkok Royal Hotel, 2–12 Pilkem Street, You Ma Tei, Kowloon (tel: 2735 9181). The Jordan MTR station is very close by so the location is not a problem. There is a café and a restaurant serving very good Thai dishes. The rooms are rather basic and functional, but they are affordable. There are 70 rooms, charging rates of HK$667–HK$805.

Concourse Hotel, 20–46 Lai Chi Kok Road, Mong Kok (tel: 2397 6683). Catering for budget-conscious tourists with both Western and Chinese restaurants. Its 400 rooms are priced at HK$1,180–HK$1,357 a double.

Eaton Hotel, 380 Nathan Road, Yau Ma Tei (tel: 2782 1818). A value-for-money hotel with a business centre and restaurant serving good Asiatic cuisine. It has 392 rooms ranging in price from HK$980–HK$1,400 a double.

Grand Stanford Crowne Plaza Harbour View, 70 Mody Road, Tsim Sha Tsui East (tel: 2721 5161). Facilities at this harbour view hotel include a business centre, bars, pool and health club. The food served in its four restaurants is first class. The hotel has 594 rooms priced between HK$2,500– HK$3,250 a double.

Holiday Inn Golden Mile Hotel, 46–52 Nathan Road, Tsim Sha Tsui (tel: 2369 3111). A hotel with the full range of facilities and three restaurants, including the excellent Loong Yuen Chinese restaurant. It has 590 rooms priced at HK$1,190–HK$2,510 a double.

The colonial Peninsula Hotel has a fascinating history

Hyatt Regency Hotel, 67 Nathan Road, Tsim Sha Tsui (tel: 2311 1234). A first class hotel in the heart of Kowloon, with business centre, nightclub, bars and four restaurants; among them Hugo's, which is considered excellent. Rates for its 723 rooms range from HK$1,900–HK$2,200.

Kowloon Hotel, 19–21 Nathan Road, Tsim Sha Tsui (tel: 2369 8698). A subsidiary of the Peninsula Group of Hotels, but the rooms are not as large as its grand parent hotel. Facilities include two restaurants, coffee shop, bar and business centre. It has 705 rooms priced between HK$1,650–HK$2,100 a double.

Kowloon Shangri-La Hotel, 64 Mody Road, Tsim Sha Tsui East (tel: 2721 2111). A deluxe hotel with sumptuous decorations and all facilities – business centre, sauna, pool – and an elegant lobby with harbour view for drinks or afternoon tea. It has 719 rooms in the price range HK$1,750–HK$3,350 a double.

ACCOMMODATION

Convenient for high-flyers: the Regal Airport Hotel

Miramar Hotel, 130 Nathan Road, Tsim Sha Tsui (tel: 2368 1111). A large hotel with three wings, which has been long established. It has three restaurants and convention and business centres. Its 500 rooms range in price between HK$1,400–HK$1,900 a double.

Omni The Hong Kong Hotel, Harbour City, 3 Canton Road, Tsim Sha Tsui (tel: 2736 0088). A very popular hotel, with low-key elegance, well situated for the Star Ferry and Ocean Terminal shopping complex. The hotel has a pool, health club and three restaurants serving excellent food. Its 709 rooms are priced at HK$1,900–HK$2,900 a double.

Omni Marco Polo Hotel, Harbour City, Canton Road, Tsim Sha Tsui (tel: 2736 0888). This waterfront hotel has a sports centre, health centre, pool, restaurants, including the delightful La Brasserie, and bar. It has 440 rooms in the price range HK$1,700–HK$1,900 a double.

Omni Prince Hotel, Harbour City, Canton Road, Tsim Sha Tsui (tel: 2736 1888). A harbour-fronting hotel, conveniently located, with pleasant rooms and business centre. It has 401 rooms ranging between HK$1,700–HK$1,900 a double.

Park Hotel, 61–65 Chatham Road South, Tsim Sha Tsui (tel: 2366 1371). Well situated for shopping and popular with tour-groups. It has 430 large rooms within the price range HK$1,400–HK$1,500 a double.

The Peninsula, Salisbury Road, Tsim Sha Tsui (tel: 2366 6251). Hong Kong's grand old hotel, famous for its style and service. Its five restaurants serve superb food and the lobby is a meeting place for the rich and famous. The hotel has 300 rooms in the price range HK$2,900–HK$3,800 a double.

Regal Airport Hotel, Sa Po Road, Kowloon City (tel: 2718 0333). This is the main airport hotel and is connected to the airport by a walkway for easy access. French cuisine; 385 rooms for HK$1,500 a double.

Regal Kowloon Hotel, 71 Mody Road, Tsim Sha Tsui East (tel: 2722 1818). Part of the Regal International chain of hotels, the hotel has several bars, a disco and four restaurants, one of which has excellent French cuisine. Its 592 rooms are priced HK$1,850–HK$2,200.

Regent Hotel, Salisbury Road, Tsim Sha Tsui (tel: 2721 1211). A deluxe hotel overlooking the harbour with a grand and spacious lobby. A health club, business centre and pool are among its facilities. It has five restaurants serving superb food. Price range for its 602 rooms HK$2,000–HK$2,700 a double.

Royal Garden Hotel, 69 Mody Road, Tsim Sha Tsui East (tel: 2721 5215). The central architectural theme of this hotel is a garden atrium, onto which rooms face. With 420 rooms, rates range from HK$2,200–HK$3,600 a double.

Sheraton Hong Kong Hotel & Towers, 20 Nathan Road, Tsim Sha Tsui (tel: 2369 1111). Centrally located, opposite the Peninsula Hotel, the disco and night club are very lively; and the hotel offers a business centre and pool as well as 791 rooms. Prices: HK$2,300–HK$2,750.

New Territories
Regal Riverside, Tai Chung Kiu Road, Sha Tin (tel: 2649 7878). Facilities in this new hotel include pool, health centre and disco. A hotel bus shuttle service operates to KCR Sha Tin station and downtown Tsim Sha Tsui. Rates for the 828 rooms are between HK$1,350–HK$1,750 a double.

Hostels and Guesthouses
Caritas Lodge, 134 Boundary Street, Kowloon (tel: 2339 3777). **Chungking House**, 4/5th Floors, Block A, Chung King Mansions, 40 Nathan Road, Tsim Sha Tsui, Kowloon (tel: 2366 5362). **YMCA International House**, 23 Waterloo Road, Yau Ma Tei, Kowloon (tel: 2771 9111).

NIGHTLIFE AND ENTERTAINMENT

The Performing Arts

Hong Kong today has quite a rich cultural life and very modern facilities in which to present local and international performances. Western and Chinese classical music concerts are performed by professional Hong Kong orchestras – the Hong Kong Philharmonic Orchestra and the Hong Kong Chinese Orchestra – and by visiting world-famous orchestras and soloists. Traditional Chinese operas are staged before enthusiastic audiences, and visiting troupes from China perform in regional styles. Visitors will enjoy the magnificent costume colours, the make-up, and the highly stylised movements which substitute stage props, but may find the singing styles foreign to the ear. Peking opera is often full of amazing acrobatic and martial feats, but Cantonese opera can be slow moving. If you attend a performance, do not be embarrassed about leaving after an hour if you feel that you have had enough. Chinese puppet shows are also held.

The month-long Hong Kong Arts Festival, held each year from mid-January to early February, is a cultural highlight of dance, theatre, mime and music. Every two years (1996,1998) there is a festival of Asian Arts which offers a unique opportunity to see quality music, dance and theatre from the Asian region. It is held in November and December.

Pop concerts are huge events staged at the Coliseum in Kowloon. They are attended by

Dancing and acrobatics are part of the spectacular shows often held during festivals in Hong Kong

thousands of fans, regardless of whether the performers are local Cantonese, Taiwanese or Western pop stars.

Tickets for performances can be obtained from URBTIX (tel: 2734 9009) or from the individual box offices of the City Hall (tel: 2921 2840), Arts Centre (tel: 2582 0230), Academy for Performing Arts (tel: 2584 1514), or the Cultural Centre

(tel: 2734 2009), depending on the sponsors.

Cinemas screen Western and Chinese films, but Hong Kong-made Chinese *kung fu* movies are the most popular. Films may be in the original language or sub-titled. Screening times are published daily in the English language newspapers and tickets can be booked in advance. An International Film Festival occurs each March/April.

Art exhibitions are normally held in private galleries, the Arts Centre and the Hong Kong Museum of Art.

To obtain full information of what's going on in Hong Kong and where, it is advisable to check the relevant sections of the daily newspapers, or the HKTA's publications: *Official Hong Kong Guide, Hong Kong This Week*, and *Hong Kong Diary*.

Nightlife

Hong Kong's nightlife is not as obviously flamboyant as that of Bangkok or Manila but it has very lively English-style pubs, elegant bars, strobe-lit discos, nightclubs with elaborate floor shows, hostess clubs, girlie bars, and

NIGHTLIFE AND ENTERTAINMENT

massage parlours. Wan Chai is famous for its girlie bars – but be warned, this form of companionship (sometimes of the topless variety) is often very expensive.

At the **Temple Street Night Market** in Yau Ma Tei (a short walk from the Jordan Road MTR station) visitors may wander about amid fortune tellers, food stalls, story tellers, and miscellaneous vendors or just sit and watch from one of the pavement cafés.

Check your hotel for evening dinner-dance boat cruises which are operated by tour companies.

Up-market Pubs and Bars

Hong Kong Island:

Bull & Bear, Hutchison House, 10 Harcourt Road, Central.

Captain's Bar, Mandarin Oriental Hotel, Central.

Clipper Lounge, Mandarin Oriental Hotel, Central.

Delaney's One Capital Place, 18 Luard Road, Won Chai.

Dicken's Bar, Excelsior Hotel, Causeway Bay.

The Jockey, 1st Floor, Shopping Arcade, Swire House, Chater Road, Central.

Joe Bananas, Shiu Lam Building, 23 Luard Road, Wan Chai.

Noon Gun Bar, The Excelsior, 281 Gloucester Road, Causeway Bay.

Kowloon:

Bar City, Basement 2, New World Centre, Salisbury Road, Tsim Sha Tsui.

The Blacksmith's Arms, 16 Minden Avenue, Tsim Sha Tsu.

Chin Chin Bar, Hyatt Regency Hotel, 67 Nathan Road, Tsim Sha Tsui.

Grammy's Lounge, Supreme House, 2A Hart Avenue, Tsim Sha Tsui.

Inn Bar, Holiday Inn Golden Mile Hotel, 46–52 Nathan Road, Tsim Sha Tsui.

Sky Lounge, Sheraton Hong Kong Hotel & Towers, 20 Nathan Road, Tsim Sha Tsui.

Discos

Hong Kong Island:

DD II, 38-44 D'Aguilar Street, Central.

JJ's Entertainment Centre, Grand Hyatt Hong Kong, 1 Harbour Road, Wan Chai.

Post 97, Cosmos Building, 8–11 Lan Kwai Fong, Central.

Kowloon:

Catwalk Nightspot, New World Hotel, 22 Salisbury Road, Tsim Sha Tsui.

Club Metropolitan, Chinachem Golden Plaza, 77 Mody Road, Tsim Sha Tsui East.

Falcon, Royal Garden Hotel, Tsim Sha Tsui East.

Hostess Clubs & Bars

Hong Kong Island:

Club Celebrity, 175–191 Lockhart Road, Wan Chai.

Mandarin Palace Night Club, 24–28 Marsh Road, Wan Chai.

New Tonnochy Night Club, 1–5 Tonnochy Road, Wan Chai.

Kowloon:

Club Bottoms Up, Basement, 14–16 Hankow Road, Tsim Sha Tsui.

Club Deluxe, L–301, New World Centre, Office Building, 18 Salisbury Road, Tsim Sha Tsui.

Club Bboss, Lower Ground Floor, New Mandarin Plaza, 14 Science Museum Road, Tsim Sha Tsui East.

WEATHER AND WHEN TO GO

The best time to visit Hong Kong is during the months of October to December. Clear blue skies, pleasant day temperatures – mid-20°s C (mid-70°s F) and evening lows of 15–10° C (60–50° F) – low humidity and rainfall make Hong Kong's autumn weather ideal for tourist activities.
Winter is short and mild. January and February may bring cold fronts which can reduce the temperature to around 10° C (50° F) while temperatures are known to drop to freezing in parts of the New Territories.
Rising temperatures in March and April bring heavy mists, low clouds and clammy damp. Residents turn on their wardrobe heaters to prevent mildew as their apartment walls stream

The other side of Hong Kong: the forests, mountains, parklands and vegetable fields of the New Territories

WEATHER AND WHEN TO GO

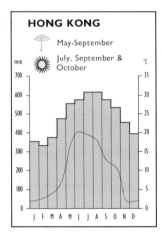

HONG KONG

May–September

July, September & October

For up-to-date information telephone the Tropical Cyclone Warning Signals Enquiries Offices (tel: 2369 0066). The hoisting of the No 3 signal requires residents to put up storm shutters and for fishing boats to make for safe harbour in typhoon shelters. The No 8 signal demands that all schools, businesses and offices close their doors to allow the public time to get home before public transport is brought to a halt. No 10, luckily rarely raised, indicates a direct hit with wind strengths of 64 knots or higher.

Clothing

Lightweight clothes are a must for summer sightseeing but a jacket or cardigan is advisable for dining out, as hotels and restaurants are air-conditioned and can be chilly. An umbrella is more useful than a raincoat during the hot months due to the high humidity.

Men may be required to wear a jacket and tie in some of the city's smart bars and restaurants. Warmer clothing – jackets, sweaters and a light overcoat – are necessary during the cooler months between December and March.

Local ladies delight in taking the opportunity of cooler weather to bring their fur coats out of cold storage, but this is a status symbol rather than a climatic necessity.

Suits are worn by Hong Kong's male business community, and the fashion-conscious young women are well dressed. However, the tourist will find casual dress both comfortable and acceptable.

with condensation. The thick mists can bring delays at airports and ferry terminals.

The long hot summer takes hold in May and continues through till August. During these months temperatures average 30–32° C (86–89° F), with little respite at night.

Humidity is high (90 per cent) and the sun strong. The monsoon season brings heavy rains, and 80 per cent of Hong Kong's rainfall occurs during these summer months, particularly in June and July.

Typhoons and severe tropical storms can plague the territory from July to September. Though it is rare to receive a direct hit, torrential downpours cause landslides and flooding and gale force winds may bring down trees and scaffolding. With their approach the Royal Observatory issues regular progress bulletins on radio and TV, and typhoon signals are hoisted throughout the territory.

HOW TO BE A LOCAL

Unlike other Asian countries, like Thailand, where traditional ways of behaviour are still the norm, in the social round Hong Kong Chinese have a Westernised sophistication. International standards of behaviour are adhered to, so that a tourist will break the ice by shaking hands, and engaging in polite exchanges about family, health, occupation and interests, just as one would elsewhere. Underneath, a traditional complicated Confucian ethic of social inter-relationships – which has dominated all Chinese societies since the 5th century BC – still exists among the Chinese themselves. However, foreigners are not expected to involve themselves in these subtleties unless they have married into Chinese families. For it is a lifetime study in itself. Hong Kong's cosmopolitanism enables the visitor to feel enveloped in an exciting and vibrant Chinese society without the distress of feeling that you are giving inadvertent offence.

A fortune teller maps out the future during the Bun Festival

SPECIAL EVENTS

Chinese Religion and Festivals

Though some Chinese are pure Buddhists, the majority practise a mixture of Taoism and Buddhism, worshipping a range of deities whose intercessionary powers are sought on the problems of daily life. The Confucian ethic of ancestor worship is very important, and most households have a family altar at which incense is burnt and offerings made regularly. In spite of the apparent modernism of Hong Kong society, it is still a very traditional one, and Chinese festivals are a colourful and

An elaborate traditional costume, with its carefully embroidered motifs and ornate head-dress

important adjunct to life, especially to New Territories villagers and boat people. Temple offerings of food (wine, roast chickens, roast suckling pig, dyed eggs, fruits) and incense are obligatory at festivals, which are always boisterous and happy occasions. Well-loved operas are performed in giant mat sheds erected for the occasion. Lion and dragon dances often form part of the celebrations. Dates of festivals are based on the lunar calendar.

The major festivals are mentioned below, but there are numerous smaller ones which are equally interesting, and it is worth enquiring through the HKTA whether there is a festival going on during your stay. Exact dates can vary widely, and a general guide only can be given.

January/February

Chinese (Lunar) New Year (late January or early February). The most important of all annual festivals, as it is a time for family reunion, ancestor worship, present-giving and feasting. The Kitchen God is sent off to report on the year's happenings (but his mouth is first smeared with sticky sweets so that he will only be flattering). All debts are paid, and red good luck couplets are placed by the doorway. New clothes are donned and visits made to friends and family. At special flower markets crowds rush to buy peach flower blossoms (representing longevity), orange trees (prosperity) and other 'lucky' flowers. Tens of thousands of Hong Kong residents return to

A Chinese juggler finds an excuse to put her feet up during a festival performance

their home villages in China for this celebration. On the second day of the New Year a huge fireworks display is held in the harbour and the city is bedecked in coloured lights, as it is for Christmas. Shops are normally closed for three days. The celebrations officially come to an end on the 15th day of the first lunar month with the hanging of paper lanterns at the Lantern Festival.

April
Ching Ming Festival. People in Hong Kong and Macau remember their ancestors on this day in early April, visiting family graves to clean them up and making offerings of food, flowers and incense before them. It is an occasion which dates back to the 3rd century BC.

SPECIAL EVENTS

April/May
Cheung Chau Bun Festival.
Dates for the festival held on
Cheung Chau Island are chosen
by divination, and celebrations
go on for seven days, culminating
in a wonderful procession in
which children are wired into
astounding postures.
Extraordinary 54-ft (16.5m) high
bun towers dominate the temple
square and nearby matsheds
house exquisite giant paper
gods. The island's inhabitants pay
homage to the God Pak Tai, Ruler
of the North, placate the ghosts,
and give thanks for surviving a
plague over a hundred years
ago. Extra ferry services are laid
on for this event.
Tin Hau's Birthday. The main
celebrations of the Empress of
Heaven are held at a temple in
Joss House Bay. Tin Hau, also
known as the Goddess of the Sea,
is the patron saint of the
fisherfolk, who come to ask her
blessings for the coming year.
Boats bedecked with silk banners
fill the bay, and more than 20,000
people take part in the festival
each year. Special ferry services
are laid on.

May
Birthday of Tam Kung. Tam Kung
is a local deity worshipped by the
fisherfolk at a temple dedicated
to him in Shau Kei Wan, Hong
Kong Island. He is believed to be
able to cure illness and subdue
the elements. Celebrations go on
throughout the day, and there is a
magnificent dragon dance.

June
Dragon Boat (Tuen Ng) Festival.
This festival is celebrated
throughout China to
commemorate the 4th-century

*The Dragon Boat Festival is now a
hugely enjoyable event, despite
commemorating a tragic death*

scholar/patriot Ch'u Yuen, who
drowned himself as a protest
against government corruption.
Boats went out in search of him
and dumplings were thrown into
the water to prevent fish from
devouring his body. The long,
narrow dragon boats can be 72ft
(22m) long and manned by up to
50 or so rowers, and a drummer
dictates the speed. Team
competition is fierce; races are
held in various parts of the
territory and special tours are
operated.

August/September

Hungry Ghosts (Yue Lan) Festival. The Chinese believe that this is the time of year when ghosts are released from Hell to roam the world and must, therefore, be placated with offerings of food, wine, paper money and incense. During the festival it is a common sight to see Hong Kong families burning prayers and money (paper offerings) by the roadside and tables formally arranged with offerings for the ghosts.

September/October

Mid-Autumn Festival. Weeks before this festival, coloured lanterns in all shapes and sizes appear in shops, making a delightful spectacle. On the evening of the mid-autumn full moon families take these lanterns with them to hill tops – usually Hong Kong Island's Victoria Peak – or beaches and parks, where they sit and watch the moon and feast on special moon cakes.

This moon-watching tradition began in the Tang Dynasty (AD618–907) but moon cakes – made of sesame seeds, ground lotus, dates and bean paste – are said to have appeared in the 14th century when messages calling for a revolt against the Mongols were put inside and smuggled to loyalists.

October

Chung Yeung Festival. In the 3rd century BC, a scholar named Huan Ching was told that, in order to avoid major calamity on the ninth day of the ninth moon, he should take his entire family to a high place and spend the day drinking chrysanthemum wine. This he did, and returning home all his livestock were dead, whereupon he immediately gave thanks. This custom has continued through the ages and has been combined with an autumn visit to family grave sites to make sacrifices of food, which are then picnicked upon.

CHILDREN

For younger members of the family, trips to Ocean Park (see **Southern District**, page 35) and the Space Museum and Science Museum (see **Kowloon**, page 41) are recommended. Otherwise there are very few facilities specifically geared towards children; but come during one of the many festivals (see **Special Events**) and they are sure to be entranced.

Even if Hong Kong is not the best-equipped place for children, its own unique charm can work wonders

TIGHT BUDGET

Hong Kong is not the easiest place to stay on a tight budget. The air fare alone can be all too hefty – but it is worth shopping around among reputable travel agents for discount fares such as APEX (Advance Purchase Excursion), which – be warned – can have several restrictions and conditions.

A few other tips might be worth keeping in mind.

● Trams are a cheap and often pleasant way of getting around, though slow. The fares are very reasonable for children. Hong Kong's public transport is not generally too costly (see **Directory** section).

● There is plenty of walking scope in Hong Kong, too: the HKTA (see **Tourist Offices**, page 123) provides details of walks.

● Hostels and guesthouses are a good idea for an economical stay (see **Accommodation**, page 97). The Hong Kong Youth Hostel Association, Room 225, Block 19, Shek Kip Mei Estate, Kowloon (tel: 2788 1638) can give advice on hostels.

● For bargain shopping, factory outlets have goods at wholesale prices, and the HKTA has a free list of member outlets.

● Eating out is not cheap – even at the street food stalls – but a bowlful of noodles, meat, vegetables and beancurd can provide a filling meal at a reasonable cost. Remember also that some restaurants make an extra charge for tea, pickles etc.

● Drinks are sold at half price in Hong Kong during 'Happy Hour' (between, 17.00 to 21.00, depending on the venue).

SPORTING ACTIVITIES

In spite of its small size, Hong Kong has many sporting facilities. Without a doubt, horse racing is the overriding passion during the mid-September to early June racing season. There are two race courses, one at Happy Valley on Hong Kong Island, and a super-modern complex at Sha Tin in the New Territories. Bets totalling more than HK$55 billion were placed in the 1991–92 season. A convenient way to attend a race meeting is to join the Hong Kong Tourist Association's HK$490 (1995–96 season) 'Come Horseracing' tour.

Taking to the sea is a natural form of escape and in the smart marinas, boating and yachting clubs, high powered sea cruisers bob alongside junks and sailing boats. The Hong Kong–Manila Yacht Race is held every other Easter. Pleasure junks can be chartered by the day or half day; for information call the HKTA (tel: 2807 6177). Other water sports which are open to visitors include water skiing, diving and wind surfing.

The Royal Hong Kong Golf Club sponsors the international Hong Kong Open Golf Championship each February at its course at Fanling, in the New Territories. Visitors may play on weekdays only at Fanling (tel: 2670 1211), at the 9-hole course at Deep Water Bay, Hong Kong Island (tel: 2812 7070), or at the Discovery Bay Golf Club on Lantau Island (tel: 2987 7271). Golfing and other sporting facilities – tennis, squash, badminton, swimming – are open to visitors at the

Sports of all kinds are readily available to tourists and locals

Clearwater Bay Golf and Country Club at Sai Kung (tel: 2719 5936) – the HKTA runs full-day tours on Tuesdays and Fridays (HK$380).

Chinese martial arts are very much the vogue, and various schools of *kung fu* are taught under the guidance of highly respected masters. For information about *kung fu*, contact the Hong Kong Chinese Martial Arts Association Ltd (tel: 2394 4803).

In spite of the overcrowding in much of Hong Kong and the New Territories, it is possible to escape for long and delightful walks in the territory's hillsides and valleys. There are now 21 designated country parks accessible by public transport. The routes are clearly signposted and well laid out with picnic and barbecue areas and nature trails. Detailed maps are on sale at the Government Publications Centre, General Post Office Building, Central (just by the Star Ferry Concourse).

Hong Kong's main beaches are supervised by lifeguards (April to October) and have changing rooms and rafts as well as barbecue areas. They are packed during summer weekends but not after the Mid-Autumn Festival in September/October. There are some very pleasant beaches, but pollution has affected some of them and the tides bring in plastic bags and debris, which are a curse.

DIRECTORY

Arriving

United Kingdom citizens do not require an entry visa for visits of up to 12 months. Commonwealth and European citizens do not need an entry visa for a stay of up to 3 months (except nationals of Finland, Germany, Greece, Iceland, also the USA, for stays of up to one month). For stays within these limits a passport only is required.

The Hong Kong Hotels Association has a counter in the airport arrivals hall and can arrange accommodation.

Hotel buses, metered taxis and airport bus services are available at the airport. There are four regular airport bus routes: No A1 services hotels in the Tsim Sha Tsui area of downtown Kowloon. The fare is HK$12. Bus No A2 crosses the harbour and services hotels in the Central District of Hong Kong Island and the Macau Terminus. The fare for this route is HK$17. The fare for Bus No A3, which services hotels in the Causeway Bay area of Hong Kong Island is also HK$14. Passengers place the fare in a collection box as they enter the bus and no change is given. These bus services operate between 06.50 and approximately midnight (tel: 2745 4466 for further details). Taxis demand a surcharge of HK$10–HK$20 if they make trips through the cross-harbour tunnels. There is also an extra charge of HK$4 per piece of luggage.

An airport departure tax of HK$50 for passengers 12 years or over is levied.

Consulates

Some 90 foreign consulates and high commissions are represented in Hong Kong. There are no embassies, as Hong Kong is still a colony. Apart from issuing visas the consulates and commissions will deal with problems such as lost passports or legal questions. Many of them have active trade sections and can advise on business potential.

A selected list follows:

Australia: 23rd/24th Floor, Harbour Centre, 25 Harbour Road, Wan Chai, Hong Kong (tel: 2827 8881)

British Immigration Department, 2nd Floor, Wan Chai Tower, 7 Gloucester Road, Wan Chai, Hong Kong (tel: 2824 6111)

Canada: 11th–14th Floors, Tower One, Exchange Square, 8 Connaught Place, Central, Hong Kong (tel: 2810 4321)

New Zealand: Room 3414, Jardine House, 1 Connaught Place, Central, Hong Kong (tel: 2525 5044)

USA: 26 Garden Road, Central, Hong Kong (tel: 2523 9011).

Customs Regulations

The duty-free allowance is: 1 litre of alcohol, 200 cigarettes (or 50 cigars or 250g of tobacco) 60 millilitres of perfume, and 250 millilitres of toilet water. Firearms and weapons must be declared and will be kept by Customs until the visitor's departure.

Driving

Traffic in Hong Kong drives on the left hand side of the road and all vehicles are right-hand drive. Road signs are written in both English and Chinese. Drivers must, however, be prepared for heavy traffic congestion, especially in the cross-harbour tunnels, and at peak hours. Hong Kong's roads seem to be constantly dug up and this, too, causes traffic delays. Hong Kong drivers are none too considerate, either. Basically, Hong Kong is being drowned in traffic, in spite of the government's attempts to restrict private motoring through steep registration and licensing fees. Parking can be a problem, though there are a number of multi-storey car parks which charge HK$13–HK$20 per hour. Metered on-street parking is common, between 08.00 and midnight on weekdays and 10.00 to 22.00 on Sundays. Parking is prohibited wherever there are no signs expressly authorising it. Many Hong Kong residents employ a chauffeur to save time and frustration. Local people like to show off their financial success with expensive cars, and Hong Kong has a high ratio of Rolls Royce and Mercedes Benz cars.

Car Breakdown

The **Hong Kong Automobile Association**, Room 405, Houston Centre, 63 Mody Road, Tsim Sha Tsui East, Kowloon (tel: 2739 5273) has an emergency breakdown service (tel: 2332 2617) which is available to all AIT-affiliated members (AA members qualify). Non-AIT members should contact the nearest garage in case of a breakdown or telephone Da Chong Hong Motor Service, who have 24-hour centres in Kowloon (tel: 2754 6222); Hong Kong (tel: 2808 6666); and Yuen Long (tel: 2479 0111).

Car Hire

The requirements for renting a car can vary from agency to agency but normally the driver must be at least 25 years of age, and have had a valid driving licence for at least two years. Some companies only accept credit cards in payment; it is best to check.

Avis (Rent A Car System Inc) Ltd, 85 Leighton Rd, Hong Kong (tel: 2890 6988).

Hertz (Rent-A-Car), Ramada Renaissance Hotel, Peking Road, Tsim Sha Tsui (tel: 2375 8779).

Electricity

Standard voltage in Hong Kong is 200 volts. All plugs are three-point but the size of the prongs varies. Most hotels have shaver points with multi-fittings, adaptors can be requested for other electrical appliances.

Emergency Telephone Numbers

In an emergency dial 999. In a medical emergency also call this number, or call the hotel doctor, or any of the following hospitals, which have 24-hour wards: Hong Kong Adventist Hospital, 40 Stubbs Road, Hong Kong (tel: 2574 6211) Queen Mary Hospital, Pok Fu Lam Road, Hong Kong (tel: 2855 3838) Queen Elizabeth Hospital, Wylie Road, Kowloon (tel: 2710 2111) The St John Ambulance Service: Hong Kong Island (tel: 2576 6555); Kowloon (tel: 2713 5555) or New Territories (tel: 2639 2555).

Entertainment Information

For current details of what's on, check the daily newspapers, the weekly publication *Orient*, the free monthly *City News*, or the HKTA's weekly *Hong Kong This Week* and *Hong Kong Diary* or monthly *Official Hong Kong*

Guide (all free), otherwise call the HKTA (tel: 2807 6177).

Health Regulations

No vaccinations are necessary unless the visitor has been in a cholera infected area within the preceding 14 days. In Hong Kong drinking water is safe to drink, especially in hotels, but many locals still prefer to boil their drinking water. In Chinese restaurants it is advisable to quench your thirst with hot Chinese tea rather than cold water.

Rides in, or pictures of, rickshaws are now a costly tourist gimmick

DIRECTORY

Holidays

There are several public holidays, and the dates of most of them vary each year: New Year's Day; Chinese (Lunar) New Year's Day and following two days (January/February); Ching Ming Festival (April); Good Friday and the day following; Easter Monday; Queen's Birthday and the Monday following (June); Tuen Ng Festival (June); the Saturday before Liberation Day; Liberation Day (last Monday in August); day following Chinese Mid-Autumn Festival (September/October); Chung Yeung Festival (October); Christmas Day; Boxing Day.

Lost Property

Should visitors be unlucky enough to lose belongings, the Police Centre at Hong Kong Side Star Ferry (tel: 2524 3447) is helpful, or call the Police Crime Hotline (tel: 2527 7177). But any police station will handle lost property enquiries.

Media

There are two English and two Chinese language commercial TV stations and six English language radio programmes. The three main local daily newspapers in English are the *South China Morning Post, Eastern Express* and *Hong Kong Standard*. Asian editions of the *Wall Street Journal* and *International Herald Tribune* are printed in Hong Kong.

Money Matters

Hong Kong's banknotes come in HK$1,000, $500, $100, $50, $20 and $10 denominations. Coins are divided into the following denominations: HK$10,

$2, $1, and 50, 20 and 10 cents. Travellers' cheques and foreign currencies are easily exchanged. It is advisable to change your money at banks rather than at hotels or money changers, for the rate is more favourable.

Hong Kong's banking hours are from 09.00 to 16.00 or 16.30 on weekdays, and to 12.30 on Saturdays.

Most major credit cards are widely accepted throughout Hong Kong.

Opening Times

Offices: 09.00 to 17.00
weekdays (to 13.00 Saturdays).
Banks: 09.00 to 16.00 or 16.30
weekdays (to 13.00 Saturdays).
Post Offices: see **Post Office**.
Shops: Usually open late and stay
open late, ie from 10.00 to 18.00
daily (though some shops close
on Sunday), but many shops stay
open until 19.30 or even 21.30.

Personal Safety

Tourists can feel relaxed
walking around and about Hong

*The well-known Star Ferry makes
its way from Central District to
Kowloon every few minutes*

Kong, even late at night.
Women on their own need not
be particularly concerned. But
one should beware of
pickpockets, especially in
crowds, and handbags should
be kept tightly under the arm.
Hong Kong residents are
required to carry identity cards,
so tourists are advised to carry
identification.

DIRECTORY

Cable cars over the headland of Ocean Park (see page 35)

Pharmacist

Chinese pharmacists abound, selling traditional herbs and remedies from ground toad cake to deer horn; many stock a wide variety of Western medicines. The main Western pharmacies include two companies which have numerous branches throughout the territory, but not all of them have dispensaries.

The largest is Watson's The Chemists, with shops in Melbourne Plaza, Hutchison House, Admiralty Centre and Prince's Building in Central District; and in the Hang Seng Bank Building, Haiphong Mansion, Nathan Tower, Harbour City, China Hong Kong City and Toyo Mall in Tsim Sha Tsui, Kowloon. Manning Dispensary has branches in The Landmark, Queensway Plaza, Regent Centre and Swire House in Central; and Harbour City in Kowloon.

Places of Worship

Anglican:
St John's Cathedral, Garden Road, Central (tel: 2523 4157)
St Andrew's, 138 Nathan Road, Kowloon (tel: 2367 1478)

Roman Catholic:
St Joseph's, 37 Garden Road, Central (tel: 2522 3992)
Rosary, 125 Chatham Road, Kowloon (tel: 2368 0980)

Others:
Methodist, 271 Queen's Road East, Wan Chai (tel: 2575 7817)
Union Church, 22A Kennedy Road, Central (tel: 2523 7247)
Kowloon Union, 4 Jordan Road, Kowloon (tel: 2369 3500)
Society of Friends (Quakers), 3rd Floor Conference Room, Mariners' Club, Middle Road, Kowloon (tel: 2368 8261)
Jewish Ohel Leah Synagogue, 70 Robinson Road, Central (tel: 2801 5442)
Baha'i, Flat C–6, 11th Floor, Hankow Centre, Middle Road, Kowloon (tel: 2367 6407)
First Church of Christ (Scientist), 31 Macdonnell Road, Central (tel: 2524 2701).

Police
Police officers wearing a red shoulder flash speak English. Emergency (tel: 999); Crime Hotline – including taxi complaints – (tel: 2527 7177); Police Enquiry Office (tel: 2866 6166).

Post Office
The General Post Office at 2 Connaught Place, Central, close to the Star Ferry Concourse (tel: 2847 1111), is open Monday to Friday 08.00–18.00, Saturday to 14.00. The main Kowloon post office is situated on the Ground Floor, Hermes House, 10 Middle Road, Kowloon (tel: 2366 4111); open Monday to Friday 09.30–18.00, Saturday to 13.00.

Public Transport
Hong Kong's transport system is varied, efficient and cheap – it needs to be, to accommodate the pressing needs of its expanding population. The picturesque traditional form of transport – the rickshaw – has died out and exists only as a tourist attraction. There are now no more than a dozen registered rickshaw men who congregate at the Star Ferry Concourse in Hong Kong side. They will run you half-heartedly around the block or pose for photographs demanding exorbitant fees which can be bargained down, but it is wise to negotiate with them beforehand.

Buses
The double-decker buses operated by the motorbus companies are, of necessity, functional – which means they are frequently overcrowded and bumpy – but services are frequent. Details of bus routes are available from the Hong Kong Tourist Association. Fares – ranging from 70 cents to HK\$22·50 – are displayed inside the bus above the coin box beside the driver. No change or tickets are given, so it is advisable to have plenty of coins if you are intending to use the buses often.

DIRECTORY

Minibuses

The cream and red 16-seater minibuses are a fast and cheap way to get around, but difficult for visitors to learn to use. The destination is displayed on the front of the vehicle in bold Chinese characters, which makes the English underneath hard to see. They will stop – traffic regulations permitting – wherever you want. To hail one just hold out your hand. To get off, just call out to the driver and pay him as you get off.

Maxicabs

These green and yellow cabs have numbers and operate on set routes. You pay as you enter and no change is given. A particularly useful Maxicab service operates every 3–8 minutes from the Kowloon Star Ferry Concourse to the shopping and hotel areas of Tsim Sha Tsui East, Kowloon.

Taxis

Taxis are still relatively cheap and are used almost as a form of public transport rather than a luxury. They can usually be hailed in the street, though in the busy business sections they are restricted by yellow lines as to where they may pick up passengers. Hotels and taxi ranks are the easiest place to find one, and the most orderly. Drivers usually understand some English but not always. A Kowloon driver will not necessarily be familiar with Hong Kong Island and vice versa. Drivers work for 12 hours at a stretch and change shifts around 16.00. Taxis are scarce then, as they are on race days. All taxis are metered and the flagfall for the red, urban taxis is HK$13 for the first 1¼ miles (2km), with a

At Wong Tai Sin Temple, joss sticks are burned, fortune sticks cast and food is offered to the gods

HK$1·10 charge for each succeeding ⅛ of a mile (0.2km). Extra charges include HK$20 for the two cross-harbour tunnels and HK$5 for the Aberdeen tunnel. There is also an extra charge of HK$4 per item of luggage. Green and white taxis only operate in the New

the eastern end of the Island to Kennedy Town in the west. The ride costs HK$1·20 (60 cents for children) and must be the best sightseeing value in the world! It is a pleasant and unhurried way to view the city. (Trams bound for Happy Valley – a branch line – will not go the full eastern journey, so check the tram's destination.) Passengers hop on at the back and alight at the front, dropping their fare into the coin box as they do so. Trams run between 06.00 and 01.00.

One of the musts in Hong Kong is a ride on the **Peak Tram** which celebrated 100 years of service in 1988. This exciting eight-minute funicular ride offers superb vistas of Kowloon and the harbour as it scales Victoria Peak to a height of 1,300ft (397m). It is used by commuters too, so there are jerky stops along the way, and long queues form at weekends and public holidays. Tickets cost HK$12 single or HK$19·40 return; the service runs every 10–15 minutes from 07.00 to midnight. A free bus service operates every 20 minutes from 09.00 to 19.00 between the Hong Kong Star Ferry and Peak Tram terminus on Garden Road.

In the New Territories a new Light Rail Transit (LRT) system operates between Tuen Mun and Yuen Long (for further information, tel: 2468 7788).

Ferries

Cross-harbour and inter-island ferries are an integral part of Hong Kong's transport system. The **Star Ferry** is the most famous. Its green and white ferries have provided the cross-harbour service between Central, Tsim Sha Tsui and Kowloon since 1898,

Territories. Their flagfall is HK$11 and HK$1 for each ⅛ of a mile (0.2km). Should you encounter problems with a driver, note the taxi number and phone the 24hr Police Hotline (tel: 2527 7177).

Trams

There is considerable affection for Hong Kong Island's 89-year-old tram system, but its survival is under debate. The double-decker trams rumble gently down between Shau Kei Wan at

DIRECTORY

and they are as much a part of Hong Kong's romantic image as any full-sailed Chinese fishing junk. The eight-minute journey costs HK$1·70 (upper deck) and HK$1·40 (lower deck). The Star Ferry operates between 06.30 and 23.30 at very frequent intervals.

Other cross-harbour Star Ferry services operate between Central and Hung Hom (07.00 to 19.20) and Tsim Sha Tsui and Wan Chai (07.30 to 23.00). Around 120,000 commuters daily use the Hong Kong Ferry (Holdings) Company double and triple-decker ferries which serve the outlying islands and outer harbour. Ferries to the islands of Lantau, Cheung Chau, Lamma and Peng Chau take approximately an hour and the deluxe class is air-conditioned and equipped with an open sun-deck.

The Outlying Districts Services Pier is on Hong Kong Island, next to the Star Ferry. If you are thinking of making an island excursion it is best to do so during the week, as the weekend boats are packed with local young excursionists. Ferry schedules are available from the HKTA. For specific information call Star Ferry (tel: 2366 2576) or the Hong Kong Ferry (Holdings) Company (tel: 2542 3081).

Trains

The **Kowloon–Canton Railway (KCR)** was opened in 1911 and was then the final leg of the London–trans-Siberia–Hong Kong rail journey. It now operates only as far as the Chinese border at Lo Wu. The Hong Kong section of the railway has since been electrified and the journey between Kowloon Station and Sheung Shui – the furthest point you can go unless you have a visa for China – takes half an hour. The trains run every 3 to 20 minutes.

A single ordinary-class ticket as far as Sheung Shui costs HK$8, and a first class ticket HK$16 (half fare for under 12s; under 3s free). Stored-value tickets, which may be purchased at the stations, can also be used on the MTR (see below). The trains are crushingly overcrowded on Sundays and holidays.

On race days, special trains run to the Sha Tin Race Course. Direct through-trains to Canton (Guangzhou) leave Kowloon Station four times a day.

Underground (MTR)

This is not a complicated system for the visitor to grasp and it is a quick and efficient way of getting about in air-conditioned comfort. It was opened in 1980, and is used by over 2.3 million commuters each day, with services between 06.00 and 01.00. The 14-station Island Line runs along the northern side of Hong Kong Island. It connects with two cross-harbour lines: the Tsuen Wan Line, from Central, serves the outer areas of Kowloon as far as Tseun Wan in the New Territories, while the Kwun Tong Line, from Quarry Bay, serves eastern Kowloon before joining the Tseun Wan Line.

Ticket machines issue electronic tickets, which must be fed into the turnstile and retained by the user, so that they can be fed into the exit turnstile. The fare structure ranges from HK$4 to HK$11 (under 12s half-price; under 3s free). Stored-value tickets (also valid for KCR) are an option. Smoking, eating and drinking is forbidden on the trains. There are no public toilets on stations.

Student Travel

Students should contact Hong Kong Student Travel Ltd, Room 1021, 10th Floor, Star House, 3 Salisbury Road, Tsim Sha Tsui, Kowloon (tel: 2730 3269).

Telephones

Because subscribers pay flat monthly rentals, individual local calls are free and one can go into any shop or restaurant and use the telephone on request (some hotels charge a fee). A phone call from a public phone box costs HK$1. For directory enquiries dial 1081.

Aberdeen makes much of its living from fish

DIRECTORY

Lantau is twice the size of Hong Kong Island but still has open spaces and peace and quiet

Time

Hong Kong is 8 hours ahead of Greenwich Mean Time and 13 hours ahead of US Eastern Standard Time.

Tipping

Most restaurants and lounge bars add a 10 per cent service charge, though it is usual to leave a little extra – about 5 per cent. Some pubs leave it to the customer's discretion. Taxi drivers, wash-room attendants and porters will anticipate a small tip.

Toilets

Public toilets can be a problem; there are not many of them, and they leave much to be desired. People usually find it best to use the toilets in the big hotels, department stores or in the Star Ferry Upper Deck entrance.

Tourist Offices

The **Hong Kong Tourist Association (HKTA)** is highly

2000 (tel: 02 251 2855).
Canada: Suite 909, 347 Bay
Street, Toronto, Ontario, M5H 2R7
(tel: 416/366 2389).
UK: 4th Floor, 125 Pall Mall,
London SW1Y 5EA (tel: 0171 930
4775).
USA: 5th Floor, 590 Fifth Avenue,
New York, NY 10036-4706 (tel:
212/869 5008).

Tours and Excursions
Tours are operated by private
companies and by the HKTA. For
information, contact the HKTA
centres (see above). Prices for
the tours may change.
Hong Kong Island tours A four-
hour morning or afternoon
excursion around Hong Kong
Island includes the beautiful
southern side of the island, the
fishing harbour of Aberdeen, and
Victoria Peak. Tour price:
HK$240 (adult), HK$160 (child).
A seven-hour day trip, at the
price of HK$320 (adult) and
HK$280 (child) includes a city
tour, Stanley Market, Victoria
Peak and lunch on a floating
restaurant in Aberdeen.
Trams can be hired privately for
an evening through MP Tours
Ltd, three times a day: 10.00 to
12.00; 13.30 to 15.30; and 15.15
to 17.15. Tickets cost HK$100 for
an adult and HK$70 for a child.
Bookings are made at the Star
Ferry piers (tel: 2845 2324 – Hong
Kong; or 2366 9885 – Kowloon).
To enjoy Hong Kong's harbour
– the busiest in the world – at
closer quarters, the Star Ferry
Company offers daily one-hour
harbour cruises: the 'Noon Day
Gun' at; 11.00 the 'Seafarers' at
12.30; the 'Seabreezes' at 14.00;
the 'Afternoon Tea' at 15.15; the
'Sundown' at 18.45; and the

organised and offers a wide
range of tourist information, its
centres are located at: Shop 8,
Jardine House, 1 Connaught
Place, Central, Hong Kong Island;
the Star Ferry Concourse, Tsim
Sha Tsui, Kowloon; and Hong
Kong International Airport (Buffer
Hall). For tourist information in
English tel: 2807 6177.
The HKTA is represented in
several countries overseas
including the following:
Australia: Level 5, 55 Harrington
Street, The Rocks, Sydney, NSW

DIRECTORY

'Harbour Lights' at 21.35. Book at the Star Ferry piers on Kowloon side or Hong Kong side. Other boat cruises in Victoria Harbour and Aberdeen fishing harbour are operated by Watertours of Hong Kong Ltd, and the Hong Kong and Yau Ma Tei Ferry Co. Cocktail and dinner cruises can be made aboard the Hilton Hotel's *Wan Fu* brigantine.

Kowloon & New Territories tours There are twice daily, five-hour tours of Kowloon, Fanling, Bird Market, and the Chinese border lookout point at Lok Ma Chau. This is an opportunity to observe the village and town life of the Cantonese and to visit a walled village or a temple. Tour price: HK$220 (adult) and HK$150 (child). The 'Land Between' tour emphasises the more traditional side of life in the New Territories – markets, a fishing village and a Chinese Buddhist temple. The price of this full day tour is HK$335 (adult) and HK$285 (child/senior); it operates Mondays to Saturdays (except public holidays).
The 'Sung Dynasty Village' tour visits a re-creation of a Sung period (AD960–1279) town where traditional handicrafts, costumes and customs are experienced. The three-hour tours cost between HK$290–HK$210 (adult) and HK$190–HK$165 (child).

Macau tours The old Portuguese colony of Macau by the Pearl River estuary, 37 miles (60km) from Hong Kong is reached by jetfoils and hydrofoils in an hour. The cobbled streets date from the 16th century, when the Portuguese first established themselves here. The South European architecture of the old part of the city is delightful. For information on tours contact the Macau Tourist Information Bureau, Room 3704, 37th Floor, Shun Tak Centre, 200 Connaught Road, Central (tel: 2540 8180). Tours from HK$520 to HK$1,180.

China tours One, two and three-day tours across the border into Guangdong province to Shenzhen, Shekou and Zhongshan and to Guangzhou (Canton) give the visitor a fleeting introduction to the People's Republic of China. Tourist visas are required for China, and China International Travel Service can arrange this (see **Travel Agencies**), but the tour must be booked several days in advance. These tours are operated daily by China Travel Service (HK) Ltd, whose branches are at 2nd Floor, China Travel Building, 77 Queen's Road Central (tel: 2525 2284) and 1st Floor, Alpha house, 27–33 Nathan Road, Kowloon (tel: 2721 1331).

Travel Agencies

American Express International Inc (tel: 2811 7000; 2811 1200)
China International Travel Service (tel: 2810 4282; 2732 5888)
HK Student Travel Ltd (tel: 2730 3269)
Hong Thai Citizens Travel Services Ltd (tel: 2544 8833; 2926 3030)
Jardine Airways Division (tel: 2868 0303)
Swire Travel Ltd (tel: 2844 8448)
Thomas Cook Travel Service
Travel Expert (tel: 2367 0126)
(HK) Ltd (tel: 2545 4399)
Wallem Travel Ltd (tel: 2821 3860).

LANGUAGE

Hong Kong has two official languages: English and Chinese (Cantonese). English is spoken widely by the foreign community and in business circles, but not every Chinese person will necessarily understand English, as many have come to live in Hong Kong from mainland China.

Bright lights and a lively nightlife in Wan Chai

The local Chinese community speaks Cantonese, the dialect spoken in the neighbouring Chinese province of Guangdong. Mandarin (Putonghua) is becoming widespread while other Chinese dialects – Shanghainese, Hakka, Chiu Chow – may also be heard. Tourists are advised to have the hotel receptionist write destinations down in Chinese. This will avoid a lot of confusion and frustration.

LANGUAGE

A Chinese medicine shop. Treatments can be thousands of years old

Glossary

can you speak English? *neih wuih mwuih gong ying mahn?*
hello (only spoken on the telephone) *wai!*
how are you? *néih hou ma?*
good morning *jóu sahn*
good night *jóu tau*
I'm sorry *deui mjyuh*
no *mhaih* or *mhou*
thank you (for a service) *mgòi*
thank you (for a gift) *dò jeh*
yes *haih* or *hou*
Hong Kong *Hèung Góng*
Kowloon *Gáu Lùhng*
The New Territories *Sàn Gaai*
The Peak *Sàn Déng*
where? *bin douh?*
how long does it take? *yiu géi nói?*
how much/how many? *géi dō?*

how much is it? *géi dō chín?*
dollar *mān*
one dollar *yāt mān*
ten dollars *sahp mān*
airport *fèi gèi chèuhng*
bus *bā sí*
Peak Tram *Laahm Chè*
tram *dihn chè*
taxi *dik sí*
what time is it? *géi dím jung?*
o'clock *dím jung*
three o'clock *saàm dím jung*
minute *fàn*

Numerals

1	*yāt*	20	*yih sahp*
2	*yih*	30	*sàam sahp*
3	*sàam*	40	*sei sahp*
4	*sei*	50	*ngh sahp*
5	*ngh*	60	*luhk sahp*
6	*luhk*	70	*chát sahp*
7	*chát*	80	*baat sahp*
8	*baat*	90	*gáu sahp*
9	*gáu*	99	*gáu sahp gáu*
10	*sahp*	100	*yāt baak*
11	*sahp yāt*	1,000	*yāt chihn*

INDEX/ACKNOWLEDGEMENTS

Acknowledgements

The Automobile Association would like to thank the following photographers and libraries for their assistance in the compilation of this book:

AA PHOTO LIBRARY Cover Night shopping, Nathan Road, 95 Peninsula Hotel (both A Kouprianoff)

J ALLAN CASH PHOTOLIBRARY 7 Kowloon, 28 Street market, 40 Tsim Sha Tsui, 49 Sha Tin, 50/1 Golden Buddha, 52 Race Course, 74/5 Floating restaurant, 86 Tea shop, 116 Cable cars, 118/9 Joss sticks, 125 Wanchai, 126 Medicine shop

NATURE PHOTOGRAPHERS LTD. 56 Pied kingfisher, (E A Janes) 62/3 Cattle egret (P R Sterry), 64 Great egret (M E Gore), 67 Mangrove swamp (E A Janes), 69 Chinese blue magpie (M E Gore), 70 Red-whiskered bulbul (M E Gore), 72 Skipper butterfly (S C Bisserot)

CHRISTINE OSBORNE PICTURES 9 Bridegroom, 24 Calligraphy, 39 Sung Dynasty Village, 57 Cheung Chau, 58 Beach, 76 Baked mud-crab, 83 Biscuits, 88/9 Local crafts

SPECTRUM COLOUR LIBRARY 4/5 Aberdeen typhoon shelter, 12/3 Causeway Bay, 15 Flower shop, 16 Stall, 20 Hong Kong & Shanghai Bank, 23 From Victoria Peak, 31 At night, 34 Repulse Bay Temple, 36 Stanley, 42/3 Wong Tai Sin Temple, 60 Lantau Island, 73 Meat display, 79 Larder, 84/5 Repulse Bay, 92 Hollywood Road, 96 Regal Meridien Airport Hotel, 98/9 Dancers, 104 Traditional costume, 105 Jugglers, 108 Children, 110 Tennis, 113 Rickshaw, 121 Fish market

ZEFA PICTURE LIBRARY 25 Food seller, 26/7 Gardens, 32/3 Aberdeen harbour, 44 Sightseeing, 46/7 Castle Peak, 54/5 Rice fields, 80/1 Market, 91 Street market, 101 New Territories, 103 Fortune teller, 106/7 Dragon Boat Festival, 114/5 Ferry, 122/3 Lantau Island

The Automobile Association would also like to thank the **Hong Kong Tourist Association (HKTA)** for their assistance in updating this revised edtion.